Dolls in National and Folk Costume

Dolls in National and Folk Costume

JEAN GREENHOWE

B T Batsford Ltd   London

ISBN 0 7134 1042 6 (hardback)
     0 7134 1043 4 (paperback)

Filmset in 9 on 11pt. Monophoto Photina by
Servis Filmsetting Ltd, Manchester
Printed in Great Britain by
The Anchor Press Ltd, Tiptree, Essex
for the publishers B T Batsford Ltd
4 Fitzhardinge Street, London, W1H 0AH

Contents

Preface 6
Introduction 7

General instructions 8
Materials required 9
Making a basic cone doll 11
Making a male doll with legs 16
Making a female doll with legs 18
Making dolls with needle-modelled
   faces and hands 21
American Indian costume *Blackfoot* 25
Mexican costume *Tehuantepec* 29
Sicilian costume *Taormina* 34
Japanese costume 39
Indian costume 43
Spanish costume *Andalucia* 47
New Zealand Maori costume 51
French costume *Alsace* 55
Lapland costume 59
Welsh costume 65
American cowboy costume 69
German costume *Black Forest* 77
Scottish fishwife costume
   Newhaven and Fisherrow 81
London pearly queen costume 89
London pearly king costume 93
Netherlands mother costume
   Volendam 97
Netherlands fisherman costume
   Volendam 104
Netherlands child costume
   Volendam 109

Bibliography 112

Preface

The purpose of this book is essentially a practical one, that is, to describe how to make and dress dolls in costume. For those readers who would like more information on the history and evolution of folk costume a bibliography is provided at the end of the book. It must be noted here, however, that very few countries have a true 'national' costume and costumes can vary greatly in detail from region to region and village to village, especially in Europe.

Introduction

The dolls in this book are about 28 cm (11 in.) in height and they are all made from cheap and easily obtained materials. Simple cardboard cones and tubes form the bodies and legs, the heads are stuffed and made from cuttings off stretch nylon tights or stockings and the arms are pipe cleaners, padded and covered to match the heads.

After the general instructions, the first section shows how to make a simple basic cone doll without legs. This method is only suitable for costumes with full-length skirts. However, if desired *all* the female dolls in the book can be constructed in this way providing their skirts are made full-length to cover the cardboard cone of the body. Although such costumes would not be strictly authentic, the idea should appeal to those who might not wish to attempt the dolls with legs at first.

Male dolls of course do require legs and next there are instructions for adding these to the basic doll for both male and female figures. Details are also given for making the shoes from a variety of materials. Taking all these ideas one step further, the next section explains how to shape the doll's face and hands with stitches. This needle-modelling gives them a most realistic and life-like appearance.

Instructions for the individual dolls follow with patterns and diagrams for making eighteen dolls starting with the basic cone dolls and working through to those with needle-modelled faces. Since all the methods used are interchangeable the dolls can be made with either plain or modelled features according to the preference or ability of the doll maker.

All the patterns for garments and accessories are printed full size and can be traced off the pages. A minimum of sewing is involved when making the costumes, and glue is used when it is easier, or neater, to stick than to sew.

For those who may wish to make costumes from countries or regions which are not included, a bibliography is given and these books can be referred to for illustrations and information about national and folk dress. From the variety of pattern shapes given throughout the book, it should be possible for the doll maker to devise many other costumes.

General instructions

Patterns

All patterns are printed full size and can be traced off the pages onto thin writing paper. Mark all details on each of the pattern pieces then cut out the patterns.

Seams

Seams, turnings or overlaps of 3 mm ($\frac{1}{8}$ in.) are allowed on all pattern pieces unless otherwise stated. 'Join' in the instructions means seam the edges together. This can be done either by hand sewing or machine stitching as desired. All fabric pieces should be joined with right sides together unless other instructions are given. Press seams open after sewing. To do this on awkward parts of a garment such as the sleeves, slip a pencil inside and press the sleeve seam open against the pencil.

Gluing

Use a quick-drying type of glue such as UHU. The largest size tube of UHU comes complete with a narrow plastic screw-on nozzle which makes the application of tiny amounts of glue an easy matter. Note that unwanted smears of UHU on fabrics or hands can be easily removed by gently rubbing with a cloth dipped in acetone. This can be obtained from chemist shops. Care should be taken when using acetone as it is highly inflammable.

Tools

All seams can be hand sewn, so a sewing machine is not essential. The usual sewing items such as needles, pins, sewing threads and scissors are required. If possible it is best to keep an old pair of scissors for cutting card and a good sharp pair for cutting fabrics. A ruler and tape measure with metric or imperial measurements are also required.

Display stands

The cardboard cone dolls will stand without support as will the dolls with shoes made from modelling clay.

However, a firm base is necessary for three of the dolls in this book and instructions are given for making the stands along with the individual dolls. These stands can of course be used for any of the other dolls if desired.

Measurements

All measurements have been worked out individually both in metric and imperial so that, in many instances, the two measurements given are not absolutely accurate conversions of each other. This has been done to avoid having awkward sizes where in fact a little extra either way will make no difference to the appearance of the finished doll. The reader can use either metric or imperial as desired.

Materials required for the basic dolls and the costumes

Card

Thin card is used for the bodies and legs. It should be flexible enough to be rolled up but strong enough to hold its shape. The type of card used for the large boxes in which food is packed (for example breakfast cereal packets) is exactly right. Alternatively, large sheets of similar card can be purchased fairly cheaply from art and craft shops.

Stuffing

This is required for padding out the dolls' bodies and arms and for stuffing the heads. Cotton wool is quite suitable except when making heads and hands which are to be needle-modelled. For these it is better to use any man-made fibre stuffing since cotton wool is difficult to model into shape.

Nylon stocking fabric

Cuttings from nylon tights or stockings are used for covering the dolls' heads and hands. They should be the stretchy type, in the usual flesh and tan colours; 30 denier nylon is by far the best because it is strong enough to stand up to needle-modelling without laddering, and 30 denier tights can usually be bought quite cheaply from chain stores in a wide variety of natural shades. Any old or discarded tights or stockings will do if necessary, but care should be taken to use only the good parts without ladders or plucks. To save repetition throughout the book, fabric off tights or stockings will simply be referred to as nylon stocking fabric.

Sewing threads

White sewing thread should be used for tying the stuffing around the dolls' bodies, arms etc. For the modelled faces and hands use thread which matches the colour of the nylon fabric. Black and white threads can also be used for adding detail to the facial features.

Pencils

These are required for marking on and colouring the dolls' faces. Pencils with very thin leads are best and the most useful colours are: white, black, red, flesh and shades of brown. Moisten the pencil leads when drawing on the faces to make a more definite mark.

Materials for the dolls' hair

Embroidery or sewing threads in the appropriate shades can be used for hair. Crêpe hair is a bit harder to handle but looks more realistic. It can usually be obtained from craft shops, toy shops, or shops which sell jokes and tricks. Crêpe hair is normally very wavy when purchased but it can be straightened out by steaming in the following way. Pin the crêpe hair onto an ironing board having it stretched to pull out the waves. Now place a wet cloth over the hair and hold a hot iron just above the cloth.

Pipe cleaners

These are required for making the dolls' arms and sometimes the feet. They usually measure about 16.5 cm (6½ in.) in length and can be obtained from tobacconist shops.

Sticky tape and glue

The tape is used for securing the card when it is rolled up in to the cone and tube shapes for the bodies and legs. Glue should be an all-purpose quick-drying type such as UHU.

Materials for the dolls' shoes

Plasticine can be used for modelling the shoes but as this does not harden, the shoes would be easily damaged. The best material for modelled shoes is a self-hardening clay such as DAS Pronto. When dry, the shoes can be coloured with the type of enamel paint used for painting plastic models of aeroplanes and soldiers. Most of the female dolls in the book have black shoes which are made from cuttings off a pair of thick stretchy nylon tights.

Fabrics and trimmings for the costumes

Oddments of any fabrics, felt, trimmings, ribbons, lace, bits of jewellery and beads will be found useful. A list of materials required is not given with each doll because of the very small pieces involved. A quick read through the instructions for each garment will at once show what is required. Occasionally a few metres or yards of trimming may be needed and quantities are given in these cases.

Fabrics which may be too stiff to drape properly on the dolls should be damped with water, then coaxed and arranged into folds and left to dry.

When very narrow braids or ribbons are required for decorating the garments, note that any trimmings can be cut into narrower widths providing that the wrong side of the trimming is first coated with glue and allowed to dry. This seals the threads together so that the cut edges will not fray out. Use this method also for sealing the cut ends of ribbons and trimmings.

Marker pens

These are extremely useful for colouring small pieces of ribbon and trimmings. For example, a length of white ribbon can be instantly 'dyed' any colour, thus providing trimming for several different costumes.

Making a basic cone doll

The pattern for the cone shape is a 25 cm (9¾ in.) radius quarter circle. To draw this out, take a piece of string and knot one end round a pencil point. Tie a knot in the string 25 cm (9¾ in.) away from the pencil point. Now stick a pin through this knot and into a piece of paper. Keeping the string taught, draw out the circle as shown in diagram 1. Cut out the circle and fold it into quarters, then cut this quarter circle pattern from card. Now using this card pattern as a template draw round it onto card for each doll. Diagram 2 shows the quarter circle of card ready for rolling up.

Roll the card into a tight cone shape having the lower edge of the cone measuring about 6 cm (2½ in.) across and securing the edges with sticky tape as shown in diagram 3. For the doll's head, make a ball of stuffing about the size of a golf ball rolling it firmly between the palms of the hands. Cut a piece of double thickness nylon stocking fabric about 10 cm (4 in.) square, push the ball of stuffing in the centre then pull the edges of the nylon around the stuffing gathering them tightly together to make a smooth rounded shape. Tie sewing thread around the gathers as shown in diagram 4.

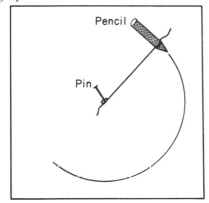

Diagram 1
How to draw out circles with a pencil and string

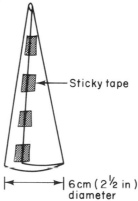

Diagram 3
The quarter circle rolled into a cone

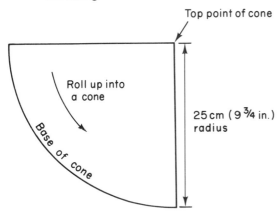

Diagram 2
The quarter circle of card

Diagram 4
Tying the stuffing inside the nylon stocking fabric

11

The head should now be slightly smaller than a golf ball and measure about 11 cm (4¼ in.) in circumference. Trim off the excess fabric close to the tied thread. This gathered portion will be at the back of the doll's head and covered by the hair or head-dress later on. Now snip a small hole in the head at the position shown in diagram 5 and push the point of a pencil inside the head twisting it round and round to open up the stuffing.

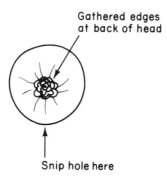

Gathered edges
at back of head

Snip hole here

Diagram 5
The back of the
head

Spread the top pointed end of the cardboard cone with glue and push it inside the head at the opening. The raw edges of the nylon fabric will be turned inwards as this is done and therefore will not fray or ladder. Now coax the face into an oval shape and pull the chin downwards with the point of a pin as shown in diagram 6. At this stage the head can be

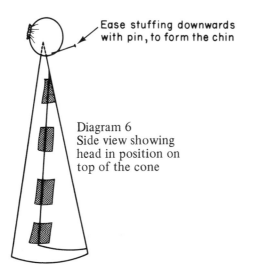

Ease stuffing downwards
with pin, to form the chin

Diagram 6
Side view showing
head in position on
top of the cone

tilted to one side if desired. Now using a well sharpened ordinary lead pencil, lightly mark on the positions of the features. An easy but most effective 'face' can be made by simply marking on dots for the eyes and several dolls in the book are made in this way. To make a perfect circle for each eye, push the moistened point of a black pencil into the face and twist it round. The eyes should be marked on about one third of the way down the face.

For a more realistic face mark on the features as shown in diagram 7. Colour the features using sharp pencils. Use black or brown for all the lines, a little red on the lips and white on the whites of the eyes. A little red colour can also be blended into the cheeks

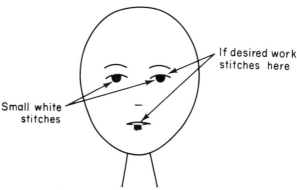

If desired work
stitches here

Small white
stitches

Diagram 7
Marking the features on the face

with a moistened fingertip if appropriate to the doll. The features can be further emphasized with a stitch or two as shown in diagram 7 using black thread above each eye and at the centre of the mouth, and white to make a tiny stitch on each eye for a 'highlight'. Take the needle through from the back of the head when making these stitches and fasten off the threads there also.

For the hair lay a few strands of thread or crêpe hair across the head and back stitch in place for a centre parting as shown in diagram 8. The hair can also be back stitched in place at one side for a side parting. Stick the strands down each side of the face and towards the nape of the neck then either trim off the strands or roll into a bun and sew in place as shown in diagram 9. Most of the female dolls in the book wear some form of head-dress which will cover the remainder of the head. A few dolls have special hair styles and details of these are given in their instructions.

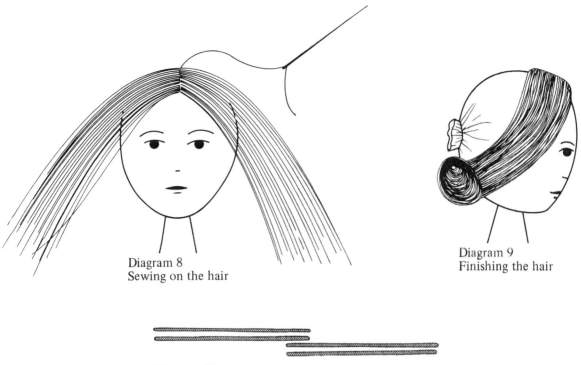

Diagram 8
Sewing on the hair

Diagram 9
Finishing the hair

Diagram 10
Lap the two pairs of pipe cleaners about 2cm (¾in.),
then tie thread round tightly to join them into one
length

For each of the doll's arms use two pipe cleaners. Join them together as shown in diagram 10. Twist the pipe cleaners together for each arm. Now using the point of the scissors, pierce a hole through the top of the cardboard cone about 2 cm (¾ in.) down from the head. Push the pipe cleaner arms through the hole so that an equal amount protrudes at each side. Spread a little glue at the centre where the pipe cleaners pass through the cone, to hold them in place.

For each hand bend round 3 cm (1¼ in.) of the pipe cleaner at the end of each arm, and make one twist to hold the bent ends of the pipe cleaners to the arms as shown in diagram 11. Pad out the hands by wrapping round a little stuffing, then cover in the same way as for the head by pulling a double thickness of nylon stocking fabric over the hands. Pull the nylon tightly up the arms then tie thread round each wrist as shown in diagram 11. Trim off the excess fabric close to the tied thread. Now pad the top of the figure, the hips and the arms by wrapping round a

little cotton wool or stuffing and tying it in place by winding round thread as shown in diagram 12. The back of the doll should be kept fairly flat and if necessary extra pieces of stuffing should be added to give shape to the chest and hips.

On some of the dolls the arms and the front of the neck will be seen and these have to be covered in a different way. To make the arm covering, trace off and cut out the arm pattern shown in diagram 13. Pin this paper pattern onto a double thickness of nylon stocking fabric which has been folded, placing the edge indicated on the pattern to the fold in the nylon fabric. Cut the nylon fabric even with the top edge of the arm pattern. Stitch close to the edge of the pattern shown by the dotted line. Remove the pattern and cut out the arm piece close to the stitching line. Turn the arm piece right side out and ease it over the doll's padded arm stretching the fabric widthways so as not to disturb the stuffing on the arm. Now stick the top edges of the arm piece onto

13

the doll's shoulders and tie a strand of thread round each arm at the positions of the wrists.

To cover the doll's neck and upper chest, stick on a small square of single thickness nylon stocking fabric stretching it round the neck towards the back of the doll. Diagram 14 shows a doll with one arm and the neck covered.

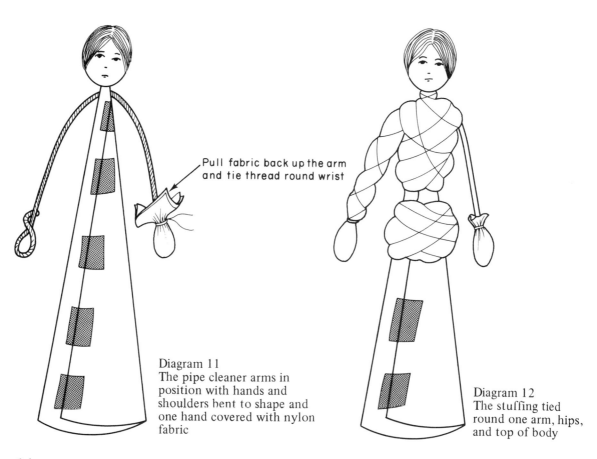

Pull fabric back up the arm
and tie thread round wrist

Diagram 11
The pipe cleaner arms in position with hands and shoulders bent to shape and one hand covered with nylon fabric

Diagram 12
The stuffing tied round one arm, hips, and top of body

14

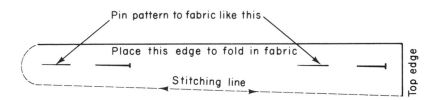

Pin pattern to fabric like this

Place this edge to fold in fabric

Stitching line

Top edge

Diagram 13
The covered arm pattern

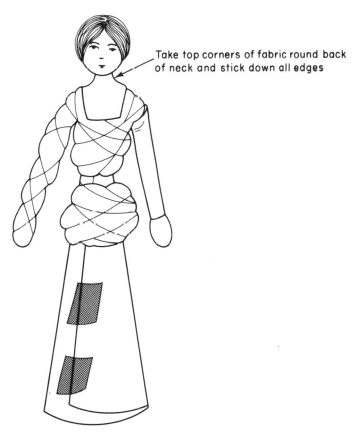

Take top corners of fabric round back
of neck and stick down all edges

Diagram 14
One arm fully covered with nylon
fabric, and neck covered at front

Making a male doll with legs

For this doll begin by making a quarter circle pattern with a 10 cm (4 in.) radius drawing it out in the same way as given for the basic cone doll. Form the card into a cone shape having the lower edge of the cone measuring about 3 cm (1¼ in.) across.

For each leg cut a 10 cm by 22 cm (4 in. by 8½ in.) strip of card. If desired, keep one strip of card as a template to draw round when making other dolls to save measuring each time. Form each of the strips into a tube by rolling the card round a pencil noting that the 22 cm (8½ in.) measurement is the length of the leg. Hold the edges of each rolled up tube in place with sticky tape and slide out the pencil. Now place the tubes together and wind sticky tape tightly round one end as shown in diagram 15, squashing the ends of the tubes flat as this is done. Spread this end

with glue and push it very firmly into the cardboard cone of the body. The overall measurement of legs and body should now be about 26 cm (10¼ in.) as shown in diagram 16.

If the shoes are to be modelled in clay they should be made next so that they can be put aside to harden while the rest of the doll is being made. Actual size diagrams of the shoes are given with each doll so that the modelled shape can be compared with the drawings on the page. Begin with two equal sized lumps of clay about 2 cm (¾ in.) in diameter. Roll them into elongated egg-shapes, then flatten slightly. Now push each of the leg tubes into the narrow ends

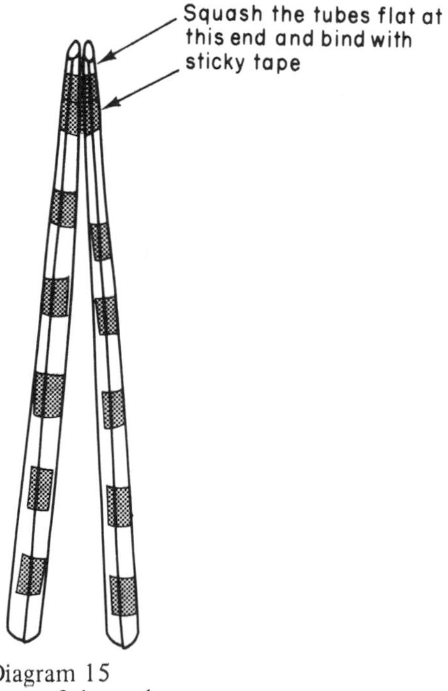

Squash the tubes flat at this end and bind with sticky tape

Diagram 15
Legs of the male doll

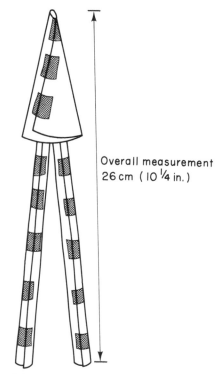

Overall measurement 26 cm (10 ¼ in.)

Diagram 16
The legs glued inside the body cone

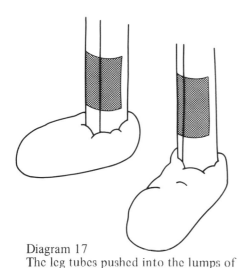

Diagram 17
The leg tubes pushed into the lumps of clay, for the shoes

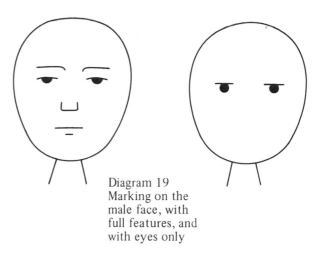

Diagram 19
Marking on the male face, with full features, and with eyes only

of the lumps of clay as shown in diagram 17. Do this so that the toes of the shoes point slightly outwards instead of forward. Push the clay well up round the ankles at the backs of the legs and shape the shoes a little more at the fronts. Normally only the toes of the shoes will be visible when a doll has trousers and therefore this shaping does not need to be very elaborate.

Pull the leg tubes carefully out of the clay and lay the shoes aside to harden while making the rest of the doll. When dry, smooth the shoes by rubbing with sandpaper, then paint them. Finally, glue the lower ends of the leg tubes into the shoes.

Because the male figure is taller than the basic cone doll the arms need to be lengthened. Do this by folding one pipe cleaner in half then join two pipe cleaners onto each end of this, lapping them 2.5 cm (1 in.) as shown in diagram 18. Now fix the arms through the body and bend and cover the hands in the same way as for the basic cone doll making the hands a little larger. Make the shoulders a bit wider and more angular when tying on the stuffing.

Make the head and fix it onto the cardboard cone in the same way as for the basic cone doll. Pull down the chin keeping it fairly square and not so pointed as for the female doll. Mark on the face as shown in diagram 19. The male dolls usually have some form of head-wear and therefore very little hair is visible. Crêpe hair is best and short lengths of this can be pulled off the piece and stuck or sewn on the head as shown in diagram 20. Leave a gap at each side of the head where the ears should be as shown. Make sure that all the bits of hair are stuck or sewn in place, then trim off all the loose ends with scissors.

Diagram 18
Lap the two pipe cleaners 2.5cm (1in.) over the folded pipe cleaner and tie them in place with thread

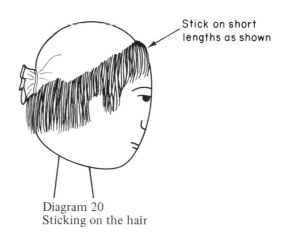

Stick on short lengths as shown

Diagram 20
Sticking on the hair

17

Making a female doll with legs

Make this in the same way as for the male doll but use 10 cm by 20 cm (4 in. by 8 in.) strips of card for the legs. After sticking the legs into the body, bring them closer together by binding a strip of sticky tape round the tops of the legs as shown in diagram 21.

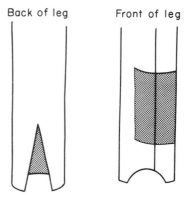

Back of leg   Front of leg

Diagram 22
First cut a V-shape at back of leg, then cut a curve at front of leg

Diagram 21
Bind the tops of the legs together with sticky tape

Some of the female dolls in the book have plain black shoes which are easy to make from cuttings off thick black nylon tights or stockings. First of all the feet have to be added to the legs. Shape the lower end of each leg by cutting away a long V-shape at the back through all thicknesses of card, and a little curved piece at the front as shown in diagram 22. This will be covered by the stockings and therefore can be done fairly roughly. On each leg bring the cut edges of the V together until they meet, then hold in place with a bit of sticky tape.

For one foot take a bundle of four pipe cleaners, fold them in half then glue all the ends of the pipe cleaners into the leg tube leaving the folded ends protruding about 3 cm (1¼ in.) beyond the end of the leg. Bend up this portion for the foot. Now stick a little stuffing along the top of each foot.

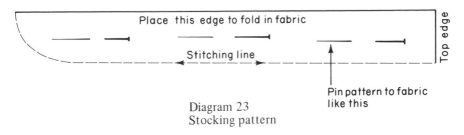

Diagram 23
Stocking pattern

Next make the stockings. Trace off and cut out the stocking pattern given in diagram 23. Pin it onto stretchy stocking fabric (details are given in the instructions for each doll) placing the edge of the pattern indicated to a fold in the fabric. Cut the fabric even with the top edge of the pattern. Stitch close to the edge of the pattern shown by the dotted line. Remove the pattern and cut out the stocking close to the stitching line. Make the other stocking in the same way. Turn them right side out then put them on the doll's legs having the seams at the centre back of the legs. Pull the stockings well up to fit the legs smoothly and stick the top edges to the doll's legs. Note that the stockings will only reach about half way up the legs.

For each shoe cut one sole and four heel pieces from thin card as shown on the patterns in diagram 24. Glue all the heel pieces together in position under the soles then glue the soles under the doll's feet as shown in diagram 25. Now, from the black stocking fabric cut two shoe pieces using the pattern shown in diagram 26 placing the upper edge of the pattern to a fold in the fabric as indicated. Keeping the shoe pieces folded, bring the short raw edges together and

Diagram 24
Patterns for shoe sole
and heel

Diagram 25
The shoe sole glued under the
foot

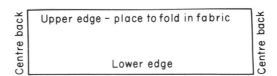

Diagram 26
The shoe pattern

19

take a small seam all round the raw edges as shown in diagram 27. Turn the shoes right side out and put them on the doll's feet stretching them to fit and having the centre back edges of the shoes at the backs of the feet. Stick in place with a spot of glue inside the heels and fronts of the shoes. Variations of this basic shape are given with instructions for the individual dolls.

Now complete the remainder of the doll, the head, arms, hands etc. in exactly the same way as for the basic cone doll, noting that the stuffing round the hips will be at the lower end of the cone and round the tops of the legs.

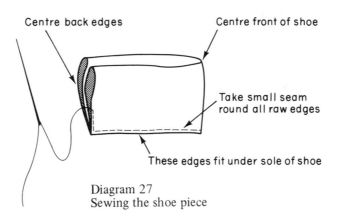

Diagram 27
Sewing the shoe piece

Making dolls with needle-modelled faces and hands

Needle-modelling of the dolls' features is not difficult but it requires a little practice to get the stitches in just the right places.

After pulling the chin downwards as instructed for the basic cone doll's head the next stage is to pull forward the stuffing at the centre of the face to form the beginnings of a nose. This is done with a needle as shown in diagram 28. Now mark points on the

together with stitches making a ridge to form the nose. Take the needle through from the back of the head to one of these marked points then take it through the nose to the other point as shown in diagram 30. Pull up the stitch then take another stitch back across the nose above and close to the first stitch. Repeat this all the way up the nose taking a little less fabric each time to get the tapered shape

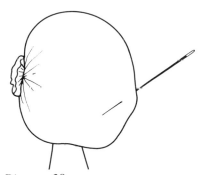

Diagram 28
Pulling out the fabric to form the nose

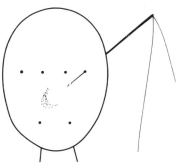

Diagram 29
Mark on these six points with pencil

face, using a sharp pencil, at the corners of the eyes and mouth as shown in diagram 29. Thread a needle with sewing cotton to match the nylon stocking fabric and knot the end of the thread. Take the needle through from the back of the head to the corner of one eye as shown in diagram 29 then take it back again leaving a tiny stitch which, when the thread is pulled, will make a small depression in the face. Oversew a couple of times at the back of the head to hold the pulled stitch in position. Now repeat this with all the points marked on the face, taking the thread through from the back of the head each time.

To make the nose, two points should be marked at either side of the base of the nose. Keep these points fairly wide apart because they will be pulled close

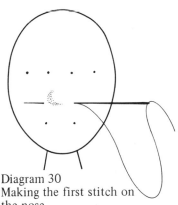

Diagram 30
Making the first stitch on the nose

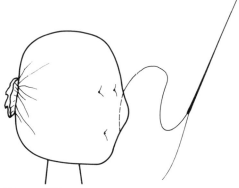

Diagram 31
Making the nose stitches

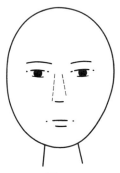

Diagram 33
Drawing on the features

shown in diagram 31. Take the thread through to the back of the head and fasten off by oversewing.

Now take a stitch through from the top of the head to the base of the nose, take it back again to the top of the head as shown in diagram 32, then fasten off.

a few tiny stitches may be added to emphasize the eyes, black for the centres and brown along the upper edges. If first attempts are unsatisfactory then the colour can be gently washed off the doll's face using a damp cloth and a little soap, providing the face is stuffed with washable man-made fibre stuffing.

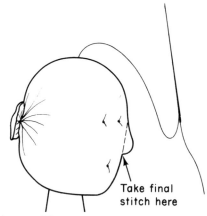

Diagram 32
Making the final nose stitch

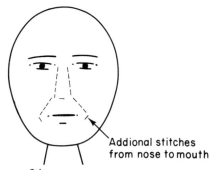

Diagram 34
Making additional stitches on a male head

The features can now be drawn in as shown in diagram 33 using coloured pencils. It helps to blend the colours into the fabric if the face is damped a little with water. Draw the centres of the eyes first then fill in the whites of the eyes. Outline the eyes lightly with black or dark brown and draw on the eyebrows. Mark the upper lip in a darker shade than the lower lip and draw a small dark line under the lower lip. Blend a little colour into the cheeks. White and flesh are very useful colours for blending in on top of other colours to tone them down. If desired,

This will not affect the needle-modelling.

For a male face, begin with exactly the same basic facial stitches but keep the chin square and try to make the nose a little larger. Additional stitches which will make a more masculine face are shown in diagram 34. These run down from each side of the nose to the corners of the mouth. The ears can be omitted if desired, leaving only small gaps where they would be when sticking on the hair as already described. If ears should be required they can be needle-modelled as follows. First take a stitch through

22

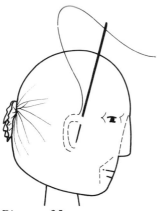

Diagram 35
Making the ears on a male
head

Diagram 37
Shaping the pipe cleaners for the
needle-modelled hands

the head from the centre position of one ear to the other, pull the thread to make small depressions and fasten off. Now doing one ear at a time, take small stitches backwards and forwards through the fabric pulling the thread tightly to form the rim of the ear as shown in diagram 35.

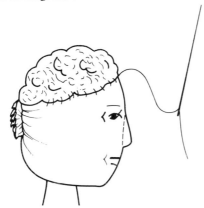

Diagram 36
Sewing a small pad of stuffing to
the top of the head

After the needle modelling is completed, the top and back of the doll's head may have become rather flat and shapeless. To rectify this, roll a small pad of stuffing and sew it securely to the head as shown in diagram 36.

The needle-modelled hands of both male and female dolls are constructed in the same way except that the male hands should be made a little larger by wrapping round more stuffing.

Bend round the pipe cleaners at the end of each arm in the same way as given for the other dolls,

but make the ends of the hands a flatter shape as shown in diagram 37. For the thumb cut a 5 cm (2 in.) length of pipe cleaner, fold it in half and tie it to the wrist of the hand with thread as shown in diagram 37. Pad out the hand by wrapping a little stuffing around it then cover the hand or the whole arm with nylon stocking fabric as required for the individual doll. Now beginning at the base of the thumb, knot the thread end and take the needle through the hand at this position. Take the needle back through again leaving a tiny stitch, pull the thread tight, then take it back through once more.

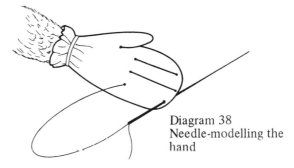

Diagram 38
Needle-modelling the
hand

This is called stab stitching. Now take the thread round the hand, between the thumb and the hand, pull the thread tight and stab stitch at the base of the thumb once more.

Pass the needle through the hand and bring it out at the position between the second and third fingers. Stab stitch through the hand at this point then pass the thread round the hand and stab stitch again as for the thumb, but this time take a little stitch through the nylon fabric at the end of the hand so that the thread does not slip off. Repeat this to make the divisions for the remaining fingers. Diagram 38 shows the final stitch being taken around the hand to divide the third and fourth fingers. The shape of the hand can be improved by squeezing, to compress the fingers against each other.

24

American Indian
costume *Blackfoot*

The dress on this doll can be made full-length and the legs omitted because in reality the feet would only just be visible. Chamois leather is the best material to use for the dress as it can be cut neatly into fringes. For the 'beadwork' decoration on the dress, braid and ribbon are used.

Doll

Make a basic cone doll using tan nylon stocking fabric for the head and also to cover the hands, arms and neck. Take care to stretch and stick the nylon fabric right around the neck as neatly as possible because the back of the neck will be seen on the finished doll. The hair, made from black felt, should be left until last. Instructions are given for this after the dress instructions.

Dress

The dress pattern is given in two pieces in order to fit it on to the page. Trace off and cut out both pieces then fix them together with a piece of sticky tape at the dotted lines A–B to make the whole pattern. Cut two dress pieces from chamois, each time placing the edge of the pattern indicated to a fold in the chamois. If the available piece of chamois is an awkward shape it may not be possible to cut out the dress pieces using the whole pattern. In this case use the patterns exactly as printed on the page then join the chamois skirt parts to the top parts by oversewing them neatly together.

On the right side of each of the dress pieces mark the dots shown on the pattern using a pencil. This is to show the positions of the fringes which will be glued on later. Snip the lower edges of the dress pieces at intervals to make a fringe about 1 cm ($\frac{3}{8}$ in.) deep.

The 1 cm ($\frac{3}{8}$ in.) wide braid which is used for the 'bead' decoration on the shoulders of the dress illustrated is white with a red diamond pattern. If a similar geometric patterned braid is not available, mark a diamond pattern on a strip of white tape or ribbon using a red marker pen.

For the 'bead' decoration across the top of the dress very narrow pale blue baby ribbon is used. Four strips of this are glued on to make up the width shown on the pattern. Alternatively one strip of ribbon about 2 cm ($\frac{3}{4}$ in.) in width can be used and the same effect obtained by making lines of stitching across it. Stick the ribbon onto each of the dress pieces then glue small strips of the diamond patterned braid down the centres of the blue ribbons as shown in the illustrations.

Now oversew the shoulder edges of the dress pieces together leaving a gap of about 4 cm (1½ in.) at the neck edge of one shoulder so that the dress can be put on over the doll's head. Join the side and under-arm edges by oversewing neatly. Turn the dress right side out and flatten the oversewn seams by stretching them gently with the fingers.

Put the dress on the doll then oversew the remainder of the open shoulder seam. Stick braid along the length of each shoulder seam. Fold a 10 cm (4 in.) strip of narrow blue ribbon in half along the length and stick. Ease it into a curved shape and glue it around the neck edge of the dress trimming off any excess length. Note that if wide blue ribbon is used for trimming the dress, a narrow strip can be cut off this instead. Now put an elastic band around the position of the doll's waist then pull up and pouch the bodice of the dress over the band. Note that the fringe at the hem of the dress should just clear the ground.

For the long fringes cut very narrow strips of chamois leather making them 9 cm (3½ in.) in length for the skirt and 7 cm (2¾ in.) in length for the top of the dress. Fold each strip in half and stick the folded ends to the dots marked on the dress. Above the folded end of each fringe, stick on a tiny red bead. To do this easily, pick up each bead with the point of a needle or pin, apply a little glue, then place in position on the dress. Thread a string of small beads and tie around the doll's neck as shown in the illustration.

Hair

From black felt, cut two hair pieces using the pattern. Cut along the dotted lines on each piece as shown on the pattern then plait these cut strips of felt and tie white thread round the end of each plait. Join the two hair pieces by oversewing them together along the back edge. Turn right side out and stretch the felt slightly making a rounded shape to fit over the doll's head. Spread a little glue on the top of the head and place the hair in position having a plait hanging down each side of the face.

For the headband, fold or cut a strip of braid to make it very narrow then stick it around the doll's head.

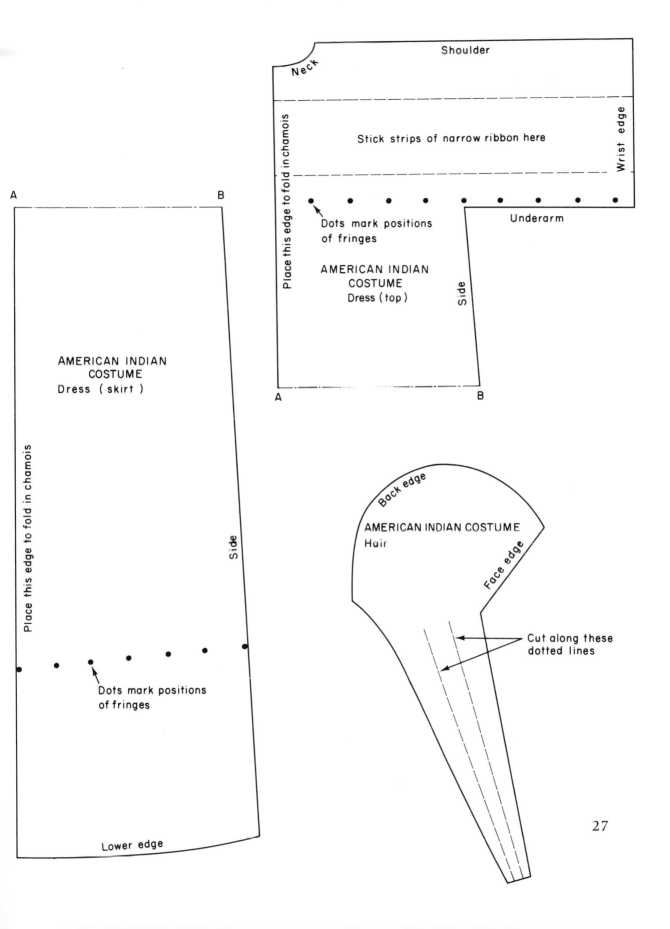

Shoulder

Neck

Place this edge to fold in chamois

Wrist edge

Stick strips of narrow ribbon here

Dots mark positions
of fringes

AMERICAN INDIAN
COSTUME
Dress (top)

Side

Underarm

A

B

A

B

AMERICAN INDIAN
COSTUME
Dress (skirt)

Place this edge to fold in chamois

Side

Dots mark positions
of fringes

Lower edge

Back edge

AMERICAN INDIAN COSTUME
Hair

Face edge

Cut along these
dotted lines

27

28

Mexican costume
Tehuantepec

30

31

The beautiful white lace head-dress on this doll is called the huipil grande. It is shaped like a baby's dress and is said to represent the dress of a baby rescued from a wreck on the coast long ago. It can be worn in two ways depending on the occasion, as shown in the illustrations. The purple cotton skirt has a white ruffle at the hem. Other suitable colours for the skirt are blue or orange printed with large floral designs. The loose fitting red blouse has a geometric border design. If floral fabric is used for the skirt, the blouse can be made from the same fabric but the geometric border should be omitted.

Doll

Make a basic cone doll and cover the hands, arms and neck. Make the hair black, with a centre parting.

Skirt

For the upper part of the skirt cut a 15 cm by 40 cm (6 in. by $15\frac{1}{2}$ in.) strip of fabric in any of the colours suggested above. For the lower part of the skirt cut a 5 cm by 40 cm (2 in. by $15\frac{1}{2}$ in.) strip of white cotton fabric. Join the pieces at one long edge and press the seam open. Turn in and stick the remaining long raw edge of the white fabric for the hem. Stick or sew on a strip of narrow lace edging 6.5 cm ($2\frac{1}{2}$ in.) above the hem edge. For the white frill at the lower edge of the dress use ready-frilled trimming 4.5 cm ($1\frac{3}{4}$ in.) in width, or gathered lace edging. Stick the top edge of the frilling to the top edge of the white fabric then use dabs of glue here and there to hold the rest of the frilling closely against the white fabric.

Join the short edges of the skirt and run a gathering thread round the top raw edge. Put the skirt on the doll, pull up the gathers round the waist and fasten off the thread. The hem of the skirt should touch the ground.

Blouse

Cut two blouse pieces from red cotton or floral fabric. For the geometric border, sew yellow tape or ribbon to one of the blouse pieces as shown on the pattern. Now sew or stick black ric-rac braid to the tape or ribbon as shown in the illustration.

Clip the neck edge of the blouse pieces as shown on the pattern then turn them in and stick, to neaten. Turn in the lower edges of the blouse pieces and stick. Join the pieces at the shoulders then at the side edges as far as points A shown on the pattern. Turn in and stick the armhole edges. Now cut a 4 cm ($1\frac{1}{2}$ in.) slit in the centre back of the blouse from the neck edge downwards so that the blouse can be put on over the doll's head. Put the blouse on the doll then overlap and stick the slit edges.

Head-dress

The lace edging on an actual huipil grande would be starched and very tightly pleated. For the doll use fairly thick lace edging about 4 cm ($1\frac{1}{2}$ in.) in width.

Cut the head-dress from thin white cotton fabric placing the edge indicated on the pattern to a fold in the fabric. Clip the neck edge then turn it in and stick to neaten. Turn in and stick the sleeve and lower edges also. For each sleeve frill cut a 6 cm ($2\frac{1}{4}$ in.) strip of lace edging. Gather slightly to fit the sleeves then lap the sleeve edges over the gathered edges of the lace and stick in place. Join the side and underarm edges including the lace.

For the frill round the lower edge of the head-dress cut a 76 cm (30 in.) length of lace edging. Join the short edges of the lace then gather it and stick all round the lower edge in the same way as for the sleeve frills.

For the frill around the neck edge cut a 2 cm ($\frac{3}{4}$ in.) wide strip off the lace edging making it about 25 cm (10 in.) in length. Join the short edges of the lace then turn in and gather the long cut edge of the lace to fit round the neck edge of the head-dress. Now stick this frill in position round the neck edge.

The illustrations show the two ways in which the huipil grande can be worn. The neck edge can be placed around the doll's face so that the sleeves hang down in front. Alternatively the lower edge of the head-dress can be draped around the face with the remainder hanging down the doll's back.

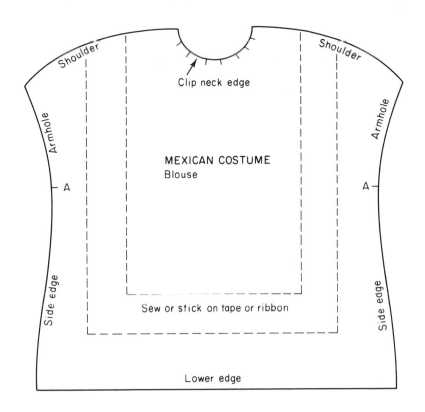

Shoulder
Shoulder
Clip neck edge

Armhole
Armhole
A
A

MEXICAN COSTUME
Blouse

Side edge
Side edge

Sew or stick on tape or ribbon

Lower edge

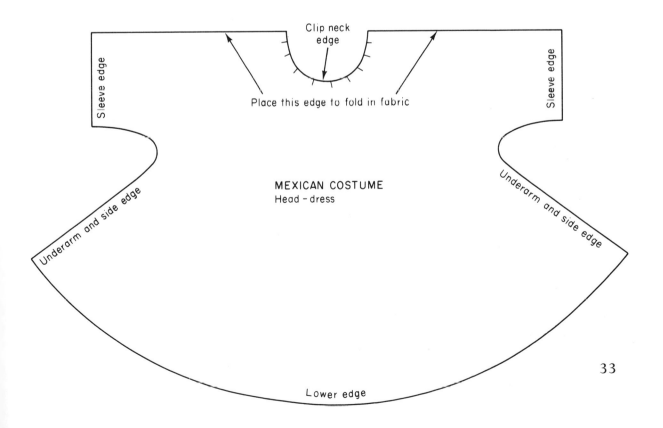

Clip neck edge

Sleeve edge
Sleeve edge

Place this edge to fold in fabric

MEXICAN COSTUME
Head – dress

Underarm and side edge
Underarm and side edge

Lower edge

33

Sicilian costume
Taormina

The bright red full length skirt is edged with blue and above this are two rows of ribbon, one gold and one silver. The yellow blouse is worn underneath a black bodice which is edged with yellow and laced up the front. The delicate white voile apron is trimmed with a frill of lace.

Doll

Make a basic cone doll and cover the hands, arms and neck. Thread a string of small red beads and tie them around the doll's neck as shown in the illustration.

Blouse

Cut the blouse from yellow fabric placing the edge indicated on the pattern to a fold in the fabric. Clip the neck edge all round as shown on the pattern. Turn in the neck edge and run a gathering thread round using black thread and starting and ending at the centre front of the blouse. Do not pull up the gathers, and take care to leave enough thread at the ends for tying in a bow when the blouse is put on the doll. Join the underarm and side edges and clip the seams at the curves. Turn in the lower edges of the sleeves and run round threads in the same way as for the neck edge.

Put the blouse on the doll taking it over the head, pull up the gathering thread round the neck and tie the thread ends in a bow. Trim off the excess lengths of thread. Pull up and tie the sleeve threads in the same way.

Underskirt

This will give shape to the skirt and it can be made from any oddment of soft cotton fabric as it will not be seen. Cut an 18 cm by 50 cm (7 in. by 20 in.) strip of fabric. Turn in one long edge and stick to neaten for the hem. Join the short edges of the strip then run a gathering thread round the remaining raw edge. Put the underskirt on the doll, pull up the gathers round the waist and fasten off. The lower edge of the underskirt should clear the ground.

Skirt

Cut a 19 cm by 50 cm (7½ in. by 20 in.) strip of red fabric. Turn in and stick one long edge to neaten for the hem. Sew a strip of 1.5 cm (⅝ in.) wide blue ribbon to the skirt having one edge of the ribbon even with the hem edge of the skirt. For the gold and silver ribbons above the blue ribbon use narrow gold and white satin ribbon. Sew the gold ribbon on about 1 cm (⅜ in.) above the blue ribbon, then sew the white ribbon 1 cm (⅜ in.) above this. Now join the short edges of the skirt, gather the waist and put the skirt on the doll in the same way as for the underskirt. The hem edge of the skirt should just touch the ground.

Apron

Cut the apron from very thin, slightly transparent fabric. Stick narrow lace to the apron as shown on the pattern. On the apron illustrated, this is a narrow strip cut off the same type of lace as that used for the frill around the edge of the apron.

For the frill use lace edging about 2.5 cm (1 in.) in width. Gather the lace and stick the gathered edge round the raw edges of the apron except for the top edge. Gather the top edge of the apron (but not the lace edging) to measure about 2.5 cm (1 in.). Stick this top edge to the top of the doll's skirt at the centre front.

Bodice

Use black felt for this. The yellow edging is narrow Russian braid but it can be omitted if desired.

Cut one back piece and two fronts. On the outside of each front piece mark the positions of the lacing-up holes with a coloured pencil. Now join the fronts to the back at the shoulders and sides, oversewing the edges together neatly. Turn the bodice right side out. Stick Russian braid round the armholes of the bodice only, the remainder is stuck on when the bodice is in position on the doll. Put the bodice on

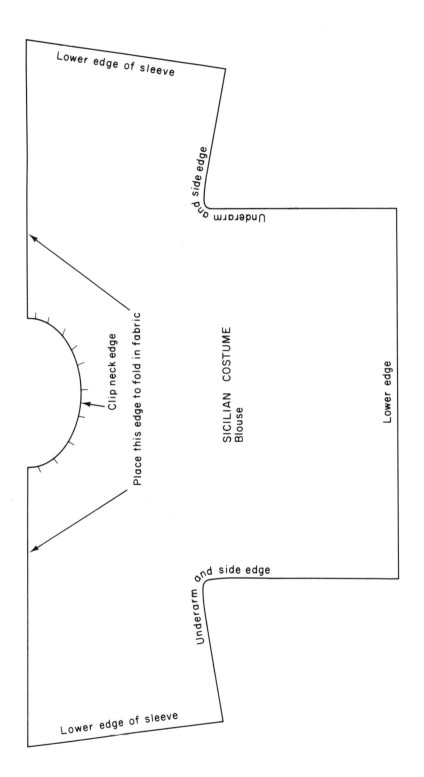

Lower edge of sleeve

Underarm and side edge

Clip neck edge

Place this edge to fold in fabric

SICILIAN COSTUME
Blouse

Lower edge

Underarm and side edge

Lower edge of sleeve

36

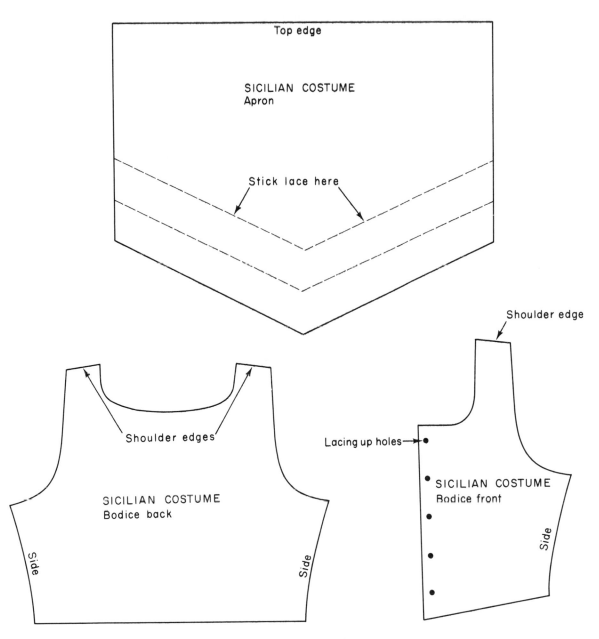

SICILIAN COSTUME
Apron

Top edge

Stick lace here

SICILIAN COSTUME
Bodice back

Shoulder edges

Side

Side

Shoulder edge

Lacing up holes →

SICILIAN COSTUME
Bodice front

Side

the doll and using two needles and a length of black thread, lace the front edges together in the same way as when threading shoe laces, taking the needles through the marked positions. Tie the thread ends in a bow at the top and trim off any excess length.

Now stick Russian braid all round the remaining edges of the bodice.

Scarf
Cut a 12 cm (4¾ in.) square of yellow fabric. Turn in and stick all the raw edges to neaten. Fold the square corner to corner, and place on the doll's head just lapping the scarf over the hair at the front. Secure two corners of the scarf at one side of the head by tying round yellow thread. Stick the remaining point of the scarf to the back of the head.

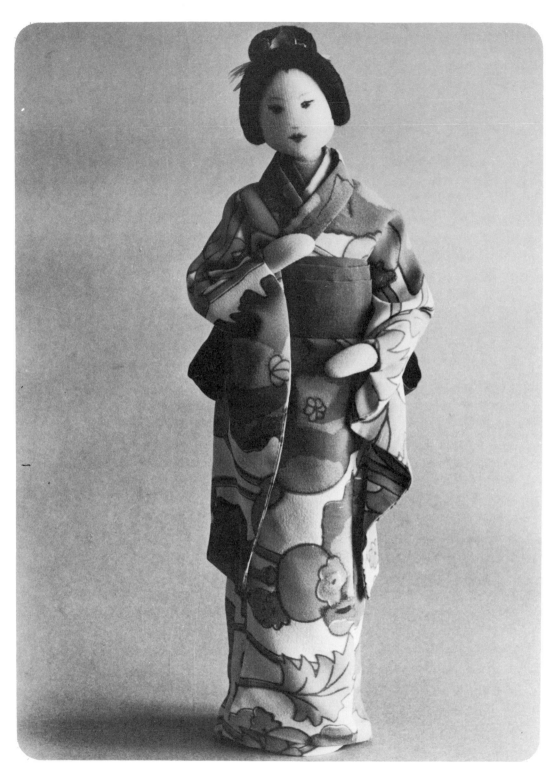

Japanese costume

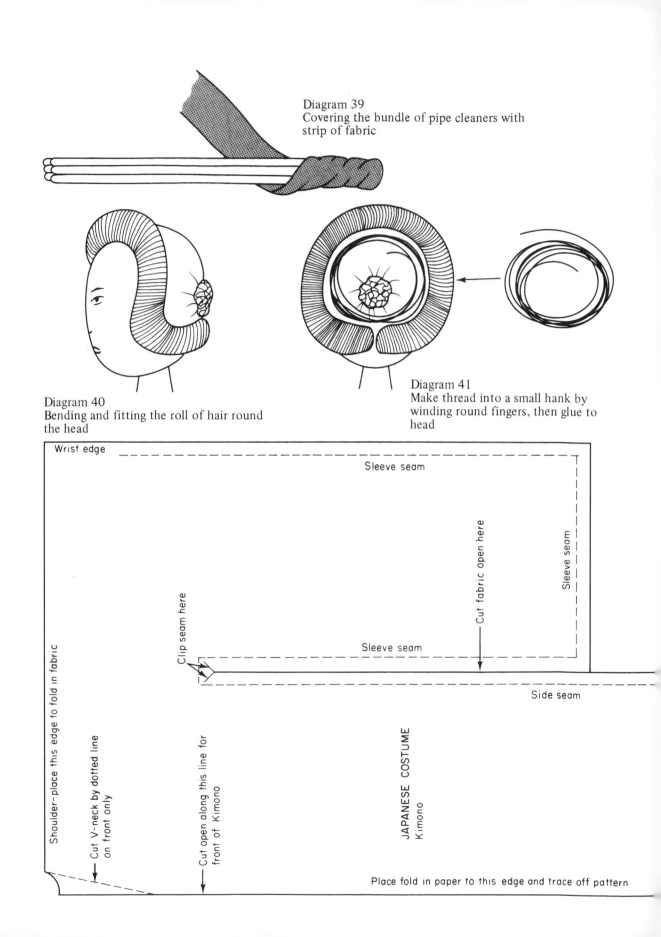

Diagram 39
Covering the bundle of pipe cleaners with
strip of fabric

Diagram 40
Bending and fitting the roll of hair round
the head

Diagram 41
Make thread into a small hank by
winding round fingers, then glue to
head

Wrist edge

Sleeve seam

Sleeve seam

Cut fabric open here

Sleeve seam

Clip seam here

Sleeve seam

Side seam

Shoulder—place this edge to fold in fabric

Cut V-neck by dotted line on front only

Cut open along this line for front of Kimono

JAPANESE COSTUME
Kimono

Place fold in paper to this edge and trace off pattern

The kimono is worn by men, women and children in Japan. It can be made from silky or cotton fabric and in practically any colour or pattern. The kimono on the doll illustrated is made from crêpe dress fabric printed with a large design in bright colours. The obi or sash can be plain or patterned.

Doll

Make a basic cone doll but tighten the cone slightly so that it measures only 4 cm (1½ in.) across at the lower edge. Use beige nylon stocking fabric for the head and also cover the hands and neck. Use the illustration as a guide when marking on the face.

The rolls of hair are made from pipe cleaners covered with black nylon stocking fabric then embroidery thread. Make the outer roll of hair first. Cut six pipe cleaners to 12 cm (4¾ in.) in length. Hold them in a bundle and wind a narrow strip of stocking fabric around to cover them as shown in diagram 39. Stick down the ends of the fabric strip. Now spread a little glue on the fabric and wind round embroidery thread to cover it completely. Bend the roll into shape to fit around the doll's head as shown in diagram 40 having the ends of the roll meeting at the back of the head. Stick the roll in place. To cover the remainder of the doll's head, wind embroidery thread around the fingers then stick in place as shown in diagram 41.

For the 'bun' of hair on top of the head, take three pipe cleaners and fold them in half. Fold twice more to make a short fat shape about 2 cm (¾ in.) in length. Cover this shape with stocking fabric and embroidery thread then stick it to the top of the head as illustrated. Glue a few dried flowers, grasses and bits of ribbon to the hair at the front of the bun.

Kimono

Only half of the kimono pattern is given in order to fit it onto the page. To make the full-sized pattern fold a piece of thin paper in half and place the fold against the line indicated on the kimono pattern. Trace off the pattern, cut it out then open up the folded paper.

Cut out the kimono placing the shoulder edge indicated on the pattern to a fold in the fabric. Cut along the lines which divide the sleeves from the body of the kimono and cut the kimono open at the centre front. Cut the V-neckline on the fronts as shown by the dotted line on the pattern. Join the side and sleeve seams as shown by the dotted seam lines on the pattern. Clip the seams at the corners and turn the kimono right side out.

Turn in the remainder of the raw edges at the wrists and press. Turn in the front and lower raw edges and stick down to neaten. Put the kimono on the doll lapping the left front over the right front. Tie a strand of thread round the kimono just beneath the doll's arms.

For the inner collar cut a 12 cm (4¾ in.) length of 1 cm (⅜ in.) wide ribbon. Stick this around the neck crossing the left side over the right side to make a V-neck at the centre front as shown in the illustration. For the kimono collar cut a 2.5 cm by 14 cm (1 in. by 5½ in.) strip of the same fabric as used for the kimono. Fold in and press the long edges to make a strip about 1 cm (⅜ in.) in width. Stick this around the neck of the kimono as illustrated, overlapping the edges at the front as for the inner collar.

Obi

Cut a 6 cm by 92 cm (2¼ in. by 36 in.) strip of fabric. Turn in the raw edges 1 cm (⅜ in.) and press, then stick them down. Fold the strip in half along the length then, beginning at the centre back, wind it three times around the doll. Stick the fabric to the doll at the back then cut off the remainder of the strip. With the remainder of the strip make a large bow and stick it to the back of the obi as shown in the illustration.

Bend the doll's arms and arrange the folds of the sleeves then stick the wrist edges of the sleeves to the doll's wrists. Stick the sleeves to the body of the kimono if necessary to make them hang down properly.

Lower edge

41

42

Indian costume

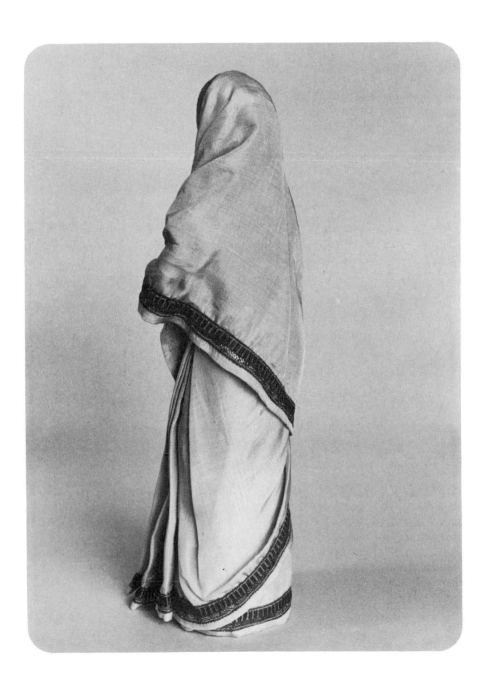

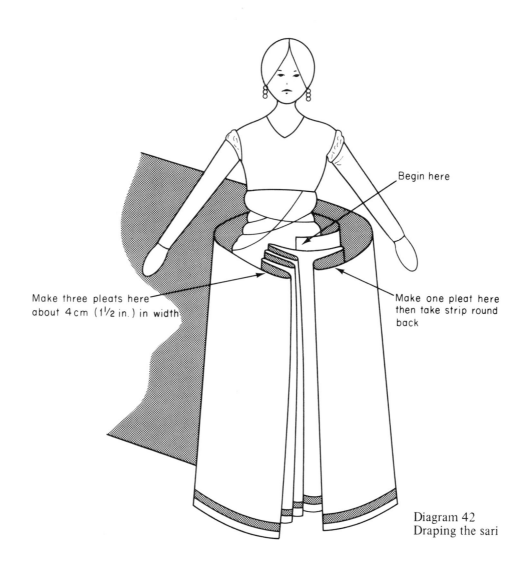

Begin here

Make three pleats here
about 4 cm (1½ in.) in width

Make one pleat here
then take strip round
back

Diagram 42
Draping the sari

1   *Top* American Indian; *left* Sicilian; *right* Mexican

2 *Top* Japanese; *left* Spanish; *right* Indian

The Indian sari consists of a strip of cotton or silk about 107 cm (42 in.) wide and over 6 metres or yards in length. It is worn over a short blouse called a choli and can be draped around the figure in a variety of ways. On the doll illustrated the choli is deep pink and the sari is lilac with a border of purple and gold braid. Decoration on a sari is usually only along the border.

Doll

Make a basic cone doll, using tan nylon stocking fabric for the head and also to cover the hands, arms and neck. Make the hair black, with a centre parting. Stick bits of gold chain to the hair at each side, for earrings. For a bracelet stick a bit of gold braid or chain around the doll's wrist.

Choli

Use white or any plain coloured cotton fabric. Only the neck of the choli will be visible on the finished doll so there is no need to make a proper blouse.

Cut out the choli using the pattern. Snip all round the neck edge as shown on the pattern then turn in the raw edges and stick down to neaten. Put the choli on the doll and stick in place having the V-neck at the centre front.

Sari

For the sari, use fabric which will crease easily such as dress lining material. A strip 18 cm (7 in.) wide by 92 cm (36 in.) in length is required and for the border, 1.3 m (1½ yd) of narrow braid or ribbon.

Make very narrow hems on all the raw edges of the strip of fabric then sew braid along one long edge and both short edges. Wet the fabric then iron it to smooth out the creases but still leave it quite damp. Now, beginning at the front of the doll, drape the sari around the waist as shown in diagram 42 forming pleats about 4 cm (1½ in.) in width at the left side. Use pins pushed through the fabric and into the cardboard cone to hold the pleats in place. Now leaving the remainder of the strip of fabric at the back of the doll, run a gathering thread round the edges of the fabric round the doll's waist through all thicknesses and pleats. Pull up the gathers to fit the waist then fasten off.

Take the remaining length of the sari up under the right arm and then across the chest to the left shoulder. Finally drape it over the doll's head to hang down over the right arm. Wet the fabric again and smooth it into natural folds and creases holding them in place with pins until the fabric is dry. Stick the sari to the doll's head to hold it in position.

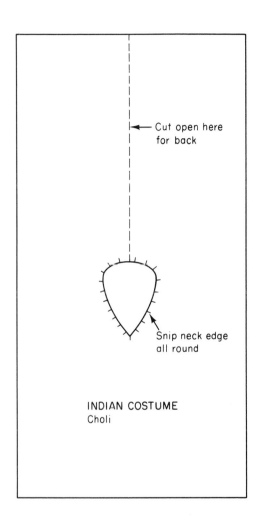

Cut open here for back

Snip neck edge all round

INDIAN COSTUME
Choli

Spanish costume
Andalucia

The dress is made from 5 cm (2 in.) wide taffeta ribbon and since the top of the dress is mostly covered by the shawl, a strip of ribbon glued to the front of the doll is the only bodice piece required. Strips of fabric can be used instead of ribbon if desired but these would have to be cut wider and the raw edges hemmed to make 5 cm (2 in.) widths. The dress is pink and the shawl bright red. Other suitable colours are blue, green, yellow and white.

Doll

Make a basic cone doll using tan nylon stocking fabric for the head and also to cover the hands, arms and neck. Make the hair black with a centre parting, then mark a curl of hair on each cheek using a black pencil. Thread a few tiny beads and tie around the doll's neck.

Dress

For the dress, 2.2 m (2½ yd) of 5 cm (2 in.) wide ribbon and the same amount of narrow lace edging are required. Cut a piece of ribbon to the length shown in the front bodice pattern then cut out the V-neck shape. Turn in the raw edges at the neck and stick down to neaten. Now stick the bodice front to the front of the doll taking the shoulder edges back over the shoulders.

Cut the skirt from an oddment of fabric placing the edge of the pattern indicated to a fold in the fabric. Mark the dotted lines on the skirt as shown on the pattern to indicate where the ribbon frills are to be glued on.

Sew the lace edging to one long edge of the ribbon then gather the other long edge to measure about 1 m (1⅛ yd). Stick the gathered edge of the ribbon to the dotted lines on the skirt to make three frills. Turn in and run a gathering thread round the waist edge of the skirt. Put the skirt on the doll having the lower frill touching the ground and the raw edges at the centre back. Pull up and fasten off the gathers then stick the waist edge of the skirt to the doll.

Now pull the ends of each frill away from the skirt to expose the centre back edges of the skirt. Overlap and stick these edges. Turn in one raw end of each frill, lap it over the other end and stick in place. Stick the pulled-away portions of the frills back onto the skirt. Finally, stick a strip of gathered ribbon round the waist edge of the skirt for the fourth frill, lapping and sticking the raw edges at the centre back as for the other frills.

Shawl

Cut a 20 cm (8 in.) square of soft, silky fabric. Fray out all the raw edges for about 2 cm (1 in.) to form the fringe, Damp the shawl, fold corner to corner and drape around the doll as illustrated. Stick in place when dry.

Comb

Cut the comb from thin card then colour it black or dark brown. Fold the lower portion back along the line indicated on the pattern and stick this to the crown of the doll's head.

Mantilla

Cut the mantilla from white lacy fabric placing the edge indicated on the pattern to a fold in the fabric. Stick narrow lace edging all round the edge of the mantilla. Damp the mantilla and drape it over the comb having the face edge along the doll's hair-line as shown in the illustration. Arrange into folds, holding them in place with pins until the lace is dry. Stick the mantilla to the doll's head at the front to hold it in place.

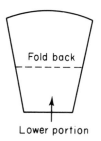

SPANISH COSTUME
Comb

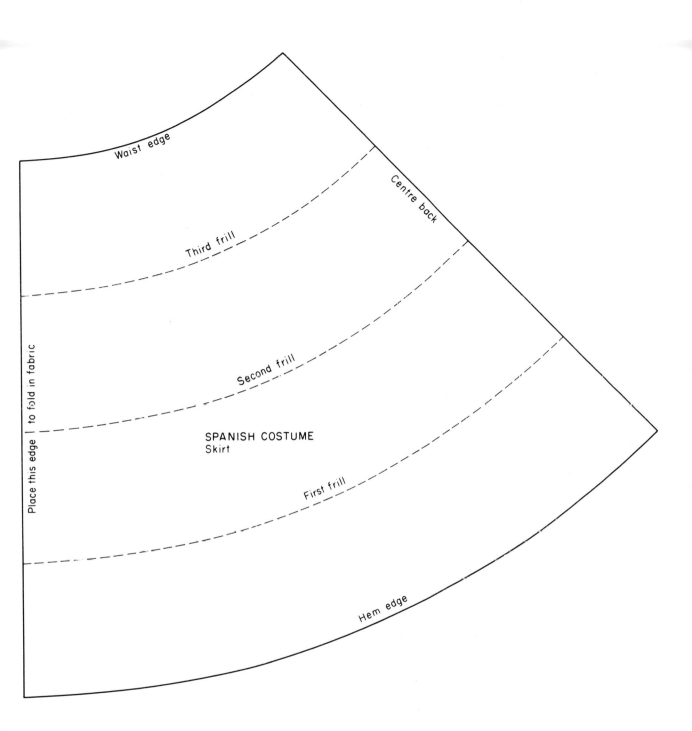

Waist edge

Centre back

Third frill

Place this edge | to fold in fabric

Second frill

SPANISH COSTUME
Skirt

First frill

Hem edge

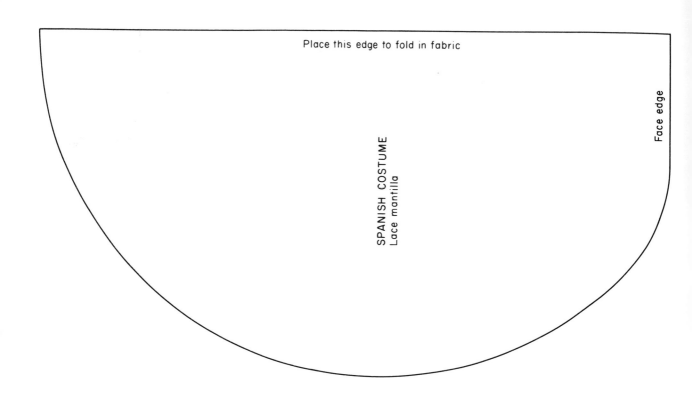

Place this edge to fold in fabric

Face edge

SPANISH COSTUME
Lace mantilla

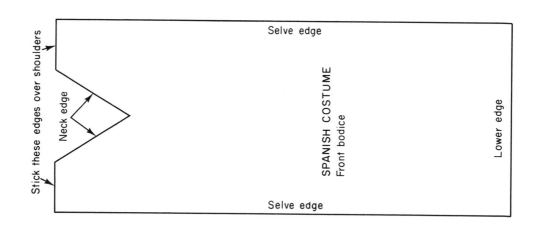

Stick these edges over shoulders

Selve edge

Neck edge

SPANISH COSTUME
Front bodice

Lower edge

Selve edge

50

New Zealand
Maori costume

The flax skirt is worn over a skirt of red fabric. A 'tiki' is worn around the doll's neck; this is a charm carved from green stone.

Doll

Make a basic female doll with legs. Use tan nylon stocking fabric for the head, hands and arms and neck. When sticking on the neck piece stretch the fabric so that it covers the upper chest also. This doll has bare legs and feet and these should be covered with tan nylon stocking fabric as though making stockings as described for the basic female doll with legs. Black crêpe hair is used for the doll's hair, and this has not been straightened out but left wavy. The hair will cover the doll's shoulders and the raw edges of the nylon stocking fabric which covers the neck and arms, but it should not be stuck in place until after the doll has been dressed.

Bodice

Cut a 6 cm by 15 cm (2¼ in. by 6 in.) strip of black cotton fabric. Turn in and stick one long edge to

neaten, for the upper edge of the bodice. Down the centre of the strip stick pieces of braid with geometric patterns in red, white, black or blue. Place the bodice around the doll and overlap and stick the short edges at the centre back trimming off any excess if necessary.

Skirt

Cut a 15 cm by 24 cm (6 in. by 9½ in.) strip of red cotton fabric. Turn in and stick one long edge to neaten, for the hem. Overlap and stick the short edges of the strip then turn in and run a gathering thread round the remaining raw edge. Put the skirt on the doll, pull up the gathers round the waist and fasten off.

Flax skirt

This is made from a piece of fawn-coloured linen fabric across which black lines are ruled, and then the fabric is frayed out. For the skirt illustrated a piece of a linen tea towel is used but any type of firmly woven fawn fabric will do. Cut a 16 cm by

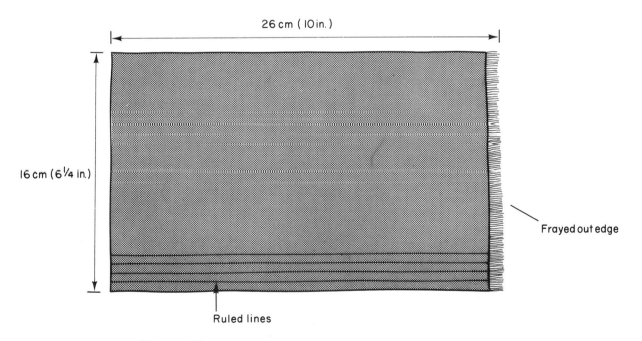

Diagram 43
Strip of fabric with one edge frayed out and a few lines ruled across it

26 cm (6¼ in. by 10 in.) strip of fabric. Fray out one 16 cm (6¼ in.) edge for about 1 cm (⅜ in.). Now rule lines at even intervals across the 26 cm (10 in.) length of the strip using a permanent black marker pen as shown in diagram 43. Mark on the lines quite heavily so that the colour penetrates the fabric as much as possible. When the lines are quite dry, fray out the strip by pulling out the threads from the frayed out 16 cm (6¼ in.) edge. Leave about 1 cm (⅜ in.) at the top edge unfrayed, for the waist edge of the skirt.

Cut a length of narrow black tape or ribbon to fit round the doll's waist for the skirt waistband. Gather the top edge of the skirt to fit the band, stick the band on to it then glue it round the doll's waist.

Tiki

This is made from a piece cut off a green wax crayon. Diagram 44 shows the actual size of the tiki on the doll and also an enlarged drawing of the shape. Use a penknife to cut and shape the piece of crayon. Tie a short length of black thread round the doll's neck and stick the tiki to the thread at the front of the doll as shown in the illustration.

Hair and headband

Sew the crêpe hair to the doll's head at the position of the centre parting, then stick it down on the head to hang over the shoulders and down the back. For the headband glue a very narrow strip of braid around the head with a small feather stuck in one side as shown in the illustration.

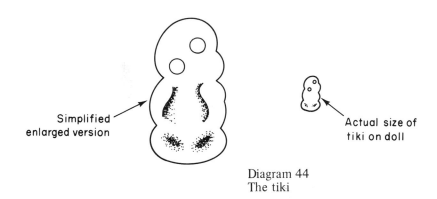

Simplified enlarged version

Actual size of tiki on doll

Diagram 44
The tiki

French costume
Alsace

56

The head-dress is a large black ribbon bow worn on the back of the head. The green silk skirt can be bordered with ribbon and braid as illustrated or left plain. The apron and fringed shawl would in reality be made of brocaded or embroidered silk, but for the small scale of the doll, printed fabric makes a good substitute. The apron can have white flowers on a black background or the other way round. The shawl is multi-coloured and edged with fringe of the type used for trimming lampshades.

Doll

Make a basic female doll with legs and cover the hands. The hair should be fair. Make the stockings from white stretchy fabric. After making the basic black nylon stocking fabric shoes, sew the top edges together almost as far as the ankles then stick on tiny black ribbon bows.

Underskirt

Cut a 14 cm by 36 cm (5½ in. by 14 in.) strip of cotton fabric. Turn in one long edge and stick to neaten, for the hem. Overlap and stick the short edges. Gather the remaining raw edge, put on the doll then pull up the gathers round the waist and fasten off.

Blouse

Cut the blouse from white cotton fabric placing the edge indicated on the pattern to a fold in the fabric. Cut the blouse open for the centre back as shown by the dotted line on the pattern. Join the underarm and side seams and clip the seams at the curves. Turn the blouse right side out, put it on the doll and overlap and stick the edges at the centre back. Run a gathering thread round each wrist edge then pull up the gathers tightly and fasten off. Gather strips of narrow lace edging and stick them round the neck and wrists to cover the raw edges of the fabric.

Skirt

Cut a 15 cm by 36 cm (6 in. by 14 in.) strip of green silky fabric. Turn in one long edge and stick to neaten, for the hem. Sew or stick two rows of narrow ribbon or braid above the hem edge as shown in the illustration. Join the short edges of the skirt then run a gathering thread round the remaining raw edge. Put the skirt on the doll, pull up the gathers round the waist and fasten off.

Apron

Cut a 14 cm by 16 cm (5½ in. by 6¼ in.) strip of fabric. Turn in and stick all the edges to neaten except for one 16 cm (6¼ in.) edge. Gather this edge to fit the doll's waist at the front. Stick the gathered edge to the centre of a strip of narrow ribbon or tape cut to fit round the doll's waist. Stick the tape or ribbon waistband round the doll's waist.

Shawl

Cut an 18 cm (7 in.) square of fabric. Turn in and stick all raw edges to neaten. Stick fringe to two adjoining edges of the shawl then fold corner to corner having the fringe trimmed edge on the outside. Turn in the folded edge of the shawl and place at the back of the doll's neck. Bring one corner across the doll's chest and glue to the waist at the side. Bring the other corner across and glue to the other side in the same way.

Head-dress

This is simply a strip of ribbon tied in a bow; 56 cm (22 in.) of black ribbon 9 cm (3½ in.) in width is used for the doll illustrated but fabric can be used instead. Turn in and stick the ends of the ribbon to neaten or, if fabric is used, cut a strip to the sizes given then turn in and stick down all the raw edges. Fold the fabric or ribbon in half along the length having the right side outside. Now tie the ribbon in a bow. Curve the bow to shape as shown in the illustration so that the loops will hang downwards, then stick it to the back of the doll's head.

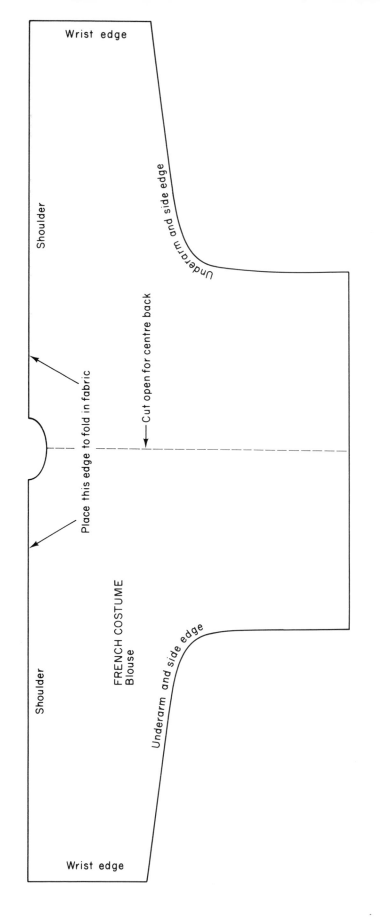

Wrist edge

Shoulder

Underarm and side edge

Place this edge to fold in fabric

Cut open for centre back

FRENCH COSTUME
Blouse

Shoulder

Underarm and side edge

Wrist edge

58

Lapland costume

The Laplanders are small people, the men being only about 150 cm (5 ft) in height. The costume shown here is of dark blue cloth trimmed with borders of red, yellow and green. The trousers of reindeer skin are tucked inside the boots which have upturned toes. The style of hat illustrated is known as the 'cap of the four winds'.

Doll

Because this figure is smaller than the other male figures, make the leg tubes 20 cm (8 in.) in length instead of 22 cm (8½ in.). Make the arms the same length as the female dolls' arms. Pad out the body, arms and hands, but do not cover the hands with nylon stocking fabric. Stick a little hair across the forehead and down each side of the face. Wrap a little stuffing around each leg and bend one leg tube at the position of the knee to pose the doll in the position shown in the illustration.

Trousers

Use fawn-coloured felt for these. Cut two trouser leg pieces, bring the centre back edges of each piece together and oversew neatly. Turn the pieces right side out, wet them, then carefully squeeze out the excess water. Slip a trouser leg over each of the doll's legs having the lower edges even with the ends of the legs. Push the trouser legs along the doll's legs to wrinkle the felt then with the point of a needle pull out the felt at the position of each knee, stretching it to make it baggy. Put the doll aside until the trousers are dry.

Boots

First make the feet with pipe cleaners in the same way as given for a female doll with legs. Wrap a little stuffing around each foot. Use fawn felt for the boots in a darker shade than the trousers. Cut out two boot pieces each time placing the edge indicated on the pattern to a fold in the felt. Oversew the back and sole edges together neatly then turn the boots right side out. Cut two soles from thin card and stick one inside each boot. Cut two boot top pieces and place one on top of each boot having the centre front points even. Now closely oversew the edges of the boot top pieces to the top edges of the boots, easing the boot edges to fit the top pieces at the points.

Place a boot on each foot, gluing the lower edges of the legs inside the boots. Using the point of a needle, stretch the front points of the boots upwards and inwards. Tie fawn or brown wool or thread tightly around the leg part of each boot, then trim the upper edge of each boot by gluing round a bit of braid.

Mittens

Use white fleecy fabric or felt for these. Cut four mitten pieces and join them in pairs round the curved edges leaving the wrist edges open. Trim the seams and turn the mittens right side out. Put one on each of the doll's hands and catch the wrist edges to the stuffing on the arms with a few stitches. Make a 'thumb' on each mitten by taking a large stitch or two round and through the mitten from point A to B as shown on the pattern. Pull the stitches up tight and fasten off.

Scarf

Use thin dark green fabric. Cut a 12 cm (4½ in.) square of fabric, fold it corner to corner and tie around the doll's neck, knotting it at the centre front.

Jacket

Use dark royal blue felt for this and the cap also. The trimmings on the jacket and cap are mainly red and yellow with a little green. Narrow braid with a geometric pattern as shown on the doll illustrated is most suitable but, alternatively, narrow ribbons and ric-rac braids could be used. For example, yellow ric-rac or ribbon could be sewn or stuck onto wider strips of red ribbon to get a similar effect.

Cut the jacket from felt placing the edge indicated on the pattern to a fold in the felt. Cut the centre front of the jacket open from the neck down the dotted line as far as point A. Now stick or sew on the braid or ribbon trimming as follows. First fix three vertical strips to the back of the jacket at the positions of the three dotted lines A—A. Next a strip to the front and back at the dotted lines B—B, cutting the trimming even with the neckline of the jacket after fixing in place. Now cut out the V-shaped neckline on the front of the jacket as shown on the pattern. Finally fix strips to the remaining dotted lines shown on the pattern.

Join the side and underarm edges of the jacket by oversewing. Turn the jacket right side out and put it on the doll. Stick braid over the slit at the front of the jacket. Cut the jacket collar from blue felt and stick on a strip of braid. Glue the collar round the neck of the jacket as shown in the illustration. Place a thread round the jacket about 7 cm (2¾ in.) above the hem edge to gather it in round the doll's waist. Tie the thread just tight enough to pouch the upper part of the jacket over the thread as shown in the illustration. For the jacket belt place a length of braid or ribbon round at the position of the tied thread and overlap and stick the ends.

Cap

For the cap band, cut strips of braid or ribbon to fit round the doll's head, then stick them together as necessary to make a 2 cm (¾ in.) width. Onto one long edge of the cap band stick a very narrow strip of white fleecy fabric or felt; this will be the lower edge. Now glue the band in position on the doll's head overlapping and sticking the short edges at the centre back.

For the top of the cap cut two pieces of blue felt using the pattern. Cut a small hole from the centre of one piece as shown by the dotted line on the pattern. Join the pieces together all round the outer edges then trim the seam and turn right side out. Now spread glue all round the top edge of the cap band and place the top of the cap on top of the band having the cut out hole against the doll's head. When the glue is dry, pull the top of the cap to one side and arrange the points as shown in the illustrations sticking them in place if necessary with dabs of glue. Cut a few lengths of very narrow red and yellow ribbon and stick to one side of the cap band as shown in the illustration.

The stand

This is made from a piece of cork cut roughly to shape with another smaller piece stuck on for the doll's left foot to rest on. Stick cotton wool to the stand for 'snow', then spread the soles of the doll's boots liberally with glue. Position the feet on the stand, then push pins through the feet and into the cork to hold in place until the glue is dry.

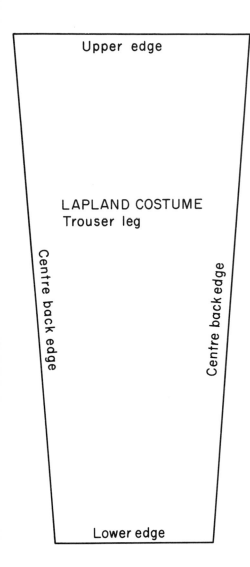

LAPLAND COSTUME
Trouser leg

Upper edge

Centre back edge

Centre back edge

Lower edge

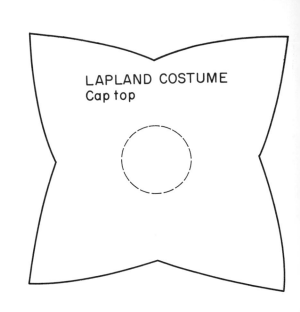

LAPLAND COSTUME
Cap top

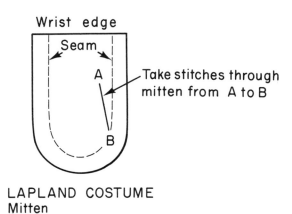

Wrist edge

Seam

A

B

Take stitches through mitten from A to B

LAPLAND COSTUME
Mitten

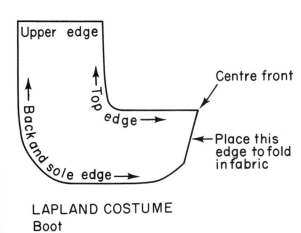

Upper edge

Top edge

Centre front

Place this edge to fold in fabric

Back and sole edge

LAPLAND COSTUME
Boot

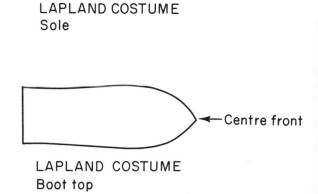

Back

Front

LAPLAND COSTUME
Sole

Centre front

LAPLAND COSTUME
Boot top

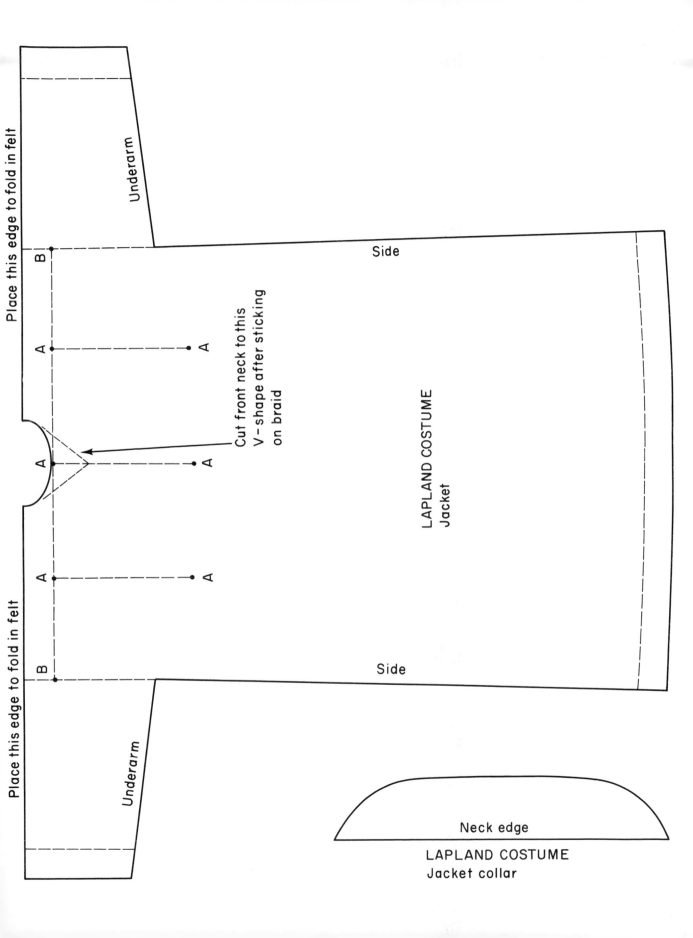

Place this edge to fold in felt

Underarm

B

Side

A — A

Cut front neck to this
V – shape after sticking
on braid

A — A

LAPLAND COSTUME
Jacket

A — A

Place this edge to fold in felt

B

Side

Underarm

Neck edge

LAPLAND COSTUME
Jacket collar

64

Welsh costume

The black beaver hat is worn over a frilled white cap which is tied under the chin. The stripes on the skirt can be black, white, blue, red or green or combinations of these colours. For the apron, white, black or checked fabric can be used. The red 'betgwn' or jacket is worn over a white blouse and a red checked shawl is draped around the shoulders.

Doll

Make a basic female doll with legs and cover the hands. Only a little hair is required at the front around the face as the rest of the head is covered by the white cap. Make the stockings from white stretchy fabric using, for example, cuttings off an old undervest or sock. Make the basic black stretchy nylon fabric shoes, then cut two small rectangles of felt for 'tongues' and glue one to each shoe. The small buckles on the tongues are made from thick fuse wire bent into square shapes and then hammered to flatten them.

Underskirt

Cut a 14 cm by 36 cm (5½ in. by 14 in.) strip of cotton fabric then turn in one long edge and stick to neaten, for the hem. Overlap and stick the short edges. Gather the remaining raw edge and put the underskirt on the doll then pull up the gathers round the waist and fasten off.

Blouse

Only the front and lower sleeves will be seen so there is no need to make a proper blouse. Use white cotton fabric. Stick a 5 cm (2 in.) square to the doll's chest just below the chin then stick a bit of white lace edging round the neck for the collar.

For each sleeve cut a 6 cm by 8 cm (2½ in. by 3 in.) strip of fabric. Stick lace edging to one short edge of each piece then overlap and stick the long edges. Run a gathering thread round each lace-trimmed edge, put the sleeves on the doll's arms, then pull up the gathers at the wrists and fasten off. Catch the top edges of the sleeves to the stuffing on the shoulders with a few stitches.

Skirt

Cut a 15 cm by 36 cm (6 in. by 14 in.) strip of fabric and make in the same way as given for the underskirt.

Apron

Cut a 14 cm (5½ in.) square of fabric. Turn in three raw edges and stick down to neaten. Gather the remaining raw edge and stick to the doll's waist at the centre front.

Betgwn

Use a fabric which will fray as little as possible. The betgwn on the doll illustrated is made from red flannelette fabric but thin felt would also be suitable. Cut out the bodice placing the edge indicated on the pattern to a fold in the fabric. Cut the bodice open at the centre front, then cut out the curved front neckline and trim off the lower corners as shown on the pattern. Turn in all the raw edges and stick down to neaten except for the side and underarm edges. Join the side and underarm edges then turn the bodice right side out. Put it on the doll then overlap and stick the centre front edges.

For the skirt part of the betgwn cut a 17 cm by 30 cm (6¾ in. by 12 in.) strip of fabric. Turn in and stick all the edges to neaten except for one long edge which will be the waist edge. Now having the side with the turned edges as the right side of the fabric, pin an inverted pleat at the centre of the skirt strip as shown in diagram 45. Turn in the raw waist edge of the skirt and run round a gathering thread. Pull up the gathers placing the skirt around the doll's waist to fit as shown in the illustration having the front edges of the skirt a little way back from the centre front edges of the bodice. Pin, then sew the gathered edge of the skirt to the bodice.

Take the front corners of the skirt and fold them back up to the centre back waist edge of the skirt. Stick the corners in place, then stick a bead for a 'button' to each one as shown in the illustration. Arrange the skirt into neat folds as illustrated.

Shawl

Cut a 12 cm (4¾ in.) square of fabric. Fray out all the edges a little then fold corner to corner and place around the doll's shoulders sticking the edges together at the centre front.

Cap

First stick on the ribbon ties. Stick a very narrow strip of ribbon to the head at each side then tie in a bow under the chin. For the cap use thin white cotton fabric. Cut out the cap using the pattern. Stick narrow lace edging to the face edge of the cap then turn in

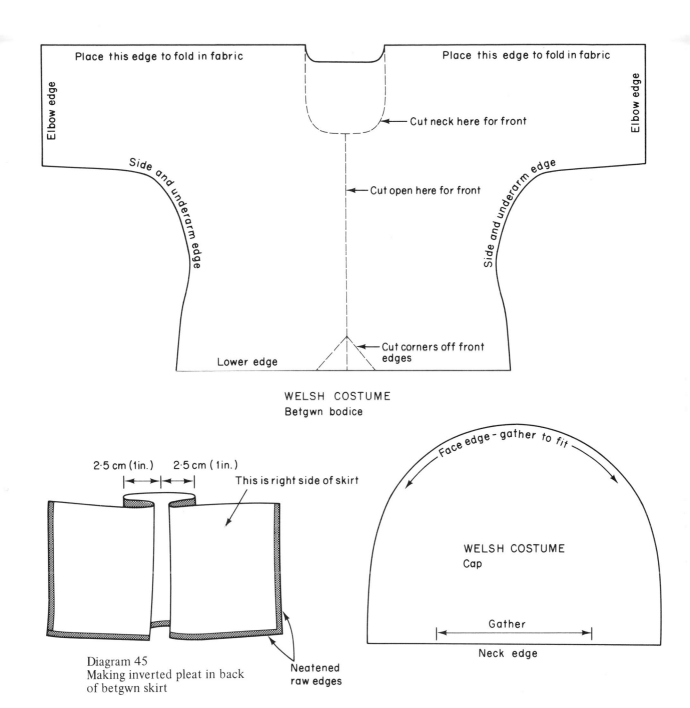

Place this edge to fold in fabric   Place this edge to fold in fabric

Elbow edge

Cut neck here for front

Side and underarm edge

Cut open here for front

Side and underarm edge

Elbow edge

Cut corners off front edges

Lower edge

WELSH COSTUME
Betgwn bodice

2·5 cm (1in.)   2·5 cm (1in.)

This is right side of skirt

Diagram 45
Making inverted pleat in back
of betgwn skirt

Neatened
raw edges

Face edge - gather to fit

WELSH COSTUME
Cap

Gather

Neck edge

and stick the back edge to neaten. Gather the face
edge to fit around the doll's face, then gather the
centre portion of the neck edge to fit the neck. Put
the cap on the doll's head and stick to the ribbons at
each side.

Hat

Use thin strong card for this, colouring it black with
marker pen. Cut out the hat brim and the crown piece
using the patterns. Bend the crown smoothly into a
cone shape bringing the straight edges together then
stick a bit of card on the inside to hold these edges
in place. Spread the top edge of the hat crown with
glue and place it on a piece of card. When the glue is
dry, cut out the card even with the crown. Stick a
bit of ribbon or tape round the lower edge of the hat
crown for a hat band.

Stick the hat brim on the doll's head on top of the
white cap at the angle shown in the illustration.
Finally, stick the hat crown on top of the hat brim.

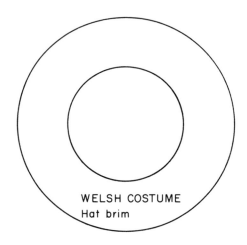

WELSH COSTUME
Hat brim

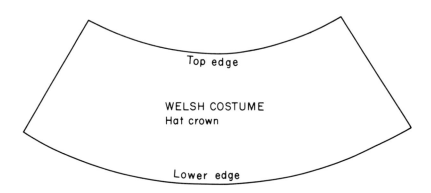

Top edge

WELSH COSTUME
Hat crown

Lower edge

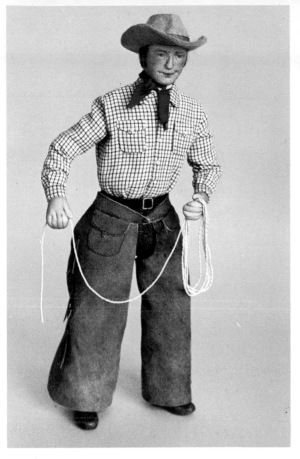

3 Cowboy

4 Scottish fishwife

5 *Left* Lapland; *right* New Zealand Maori

6 *Top* French; *left* Welsh; *right* German

American cowboy costume

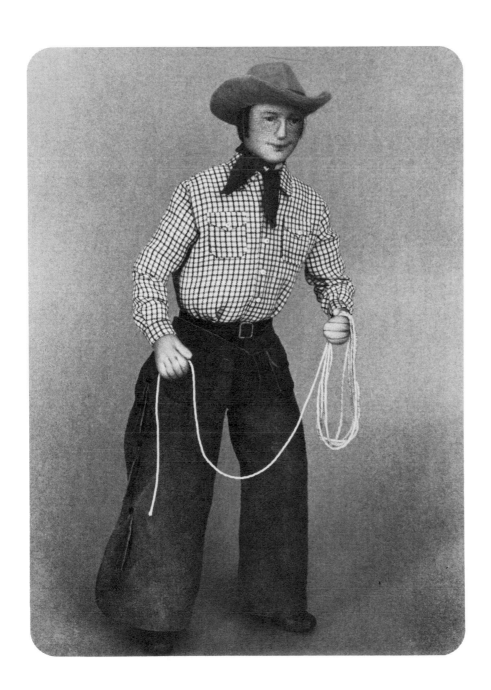

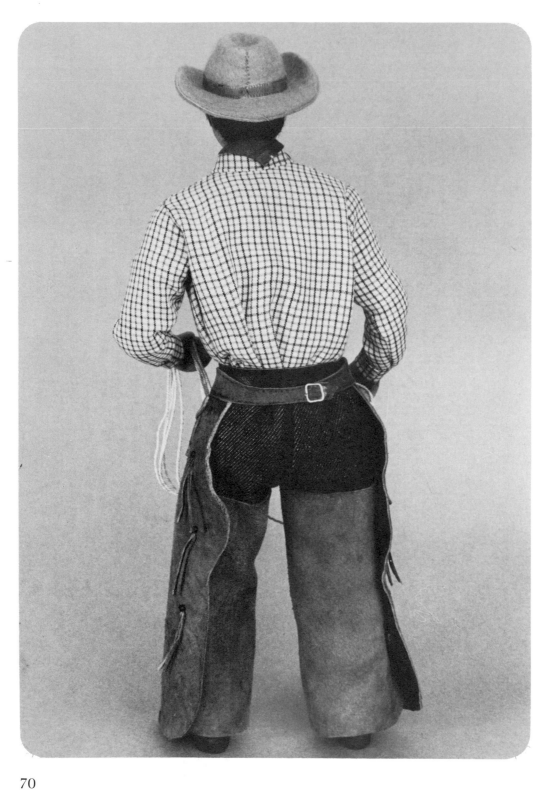

The cowboy's leather chaps are worn over blue denim jeans. The shirt is checked fabric and the neckerchief is red. A wide-brimmed hat is worn on the head and high heeled boots on the feet.

Doll

Make a basic male doll and cover the hands. Bend the left leg tube at the position of the knee to pose the doll as shown in the illustration. Modelling clay is used for the cowboy boots. First make ovals of clay as given in the basic instructions but keep the back part fairly thick because the high heel has to be modelled from this. Push the leg tubes into the ovals of clay and close the clay well up around each leg to give a good hold. Take the boots carefully off the legs and scoop out and shape the instep as shown in diagram 46. This can be done with the point of a pencil rolling it towards the sole of the boot to make the shape. Flatten the toe ends of the boots slightly and coax into shape as shown in diagrams 46 and 47.

Push the leg tubes into the boots once more to make sure they will fit then lay aside the boots to harden. When hard they can be sandpapered to shape and extra details, such as creases across the toes, can be scraped in with a penknife. Finally paint the boots light brown, but do not glue them onto the legs until the jeans are in position.

Shirt

Cut out one pair of shirt fronts and two sleeves. Cut one shirt back placing the edge indicated on the pattern to a fold in the fabric. Turn in and stick the centre front edge of each shirt front to neaten. For the pockets and flaps stick two layers of fabric together before cutting them out, to prevent the fabric fraying. Stick the pockets and flaps to the shirt fronts as shown on the shirt front pattern. Now join the shirt fronts to the back at the shoulders. Join the armhole edge of each sleeve to the armhole edges of the shirt then join the side seams of the shirt and the underarm seams of the sleeves. Turn the shirt right side out and put it on the doll. Lap and stick the left front over the right front edge.

For the collar, fold a bit of fabric and stick, forming a double layer. Place the edge of the collar pattern indicated to the folded edge of the fabric and cut out. Fold the collar along the dotted line shown on the pattern and stick it around the neck of the shirt. Cut the shirt cuffs in the same way then stick these round the wrist edges of the sleeves, overlapping and

sticking the short edges. For the shirt buttons use tiny beads, sticking them at intervals down the shirt front and to the pocket flaps. To do this easily, lift each bead on the point of a needle, apply a dab of glue, then place in position.

Neckerchief

Cut a 9 cm ($3\frac{1}{2}$ in.) square of thin red fabric. Turn in and stick all the raw edges to neaten. Fold the square corner to corner and knot it around the doll's neck as illustrated.

Jeans

Cut one pair of jeans pieces from blue denim or plain dark blue fabric. Join the pieces to each other at the centre front and centre back edges. Bring these seams together and then join the inside leg edges of each leg. Turn the jeans right side out and put them on the doll. Catch the waist edge to the shirt all round with a few oversewing stitches. For the belt cut a 6 mm ($\frac{1}{4}$ in.) wide strip of leather, or leather cloth, long enough to go round the waist plus a little extra for an overlap. Stick the belt round the waist edge of the jeans cutting the overlapped end to a V-shape. For the buckle, bend a bit of thick wire such as fuse wire into a square shape then hammer it to flatten. Glue the buckle to the belt.

Now place the ends of the leg tubes in the boots and turn up the lower edges of the jeans to suit the leg length. Do not glue the boots in place just yet.

Chaps

A piece of old, worn leather or suede can be used for the chaps, perhaps a cutting off an old garment or handbag. If a piece of new leather is available this can be rubbed, twisted and pulled to soften it and give a 'worn' look. Alternatively leather cloth or felt can be used instead.

Cut two chaps pieces and two chaps belt pieces, taking care if using leather or suede to reverse the patterns for the second pieces in order to make pairs. Cut two pockets and two pocket flaps. Stick the belt pieces to the tops of the chaps pieces as shown on the pattern noting that the front pointed end of the belt should extend about 6 mm ($\frac{1}{4}$ in.) beyond the chaps as shown in the illustration. Stick the pockets and pocket flaps on the chaps at the positions shown by the dotted lines on the pattern. If desired, mark 'stitching lines' with a black ball point pen round the edges of the belt, pockets and pocket flap pieces.

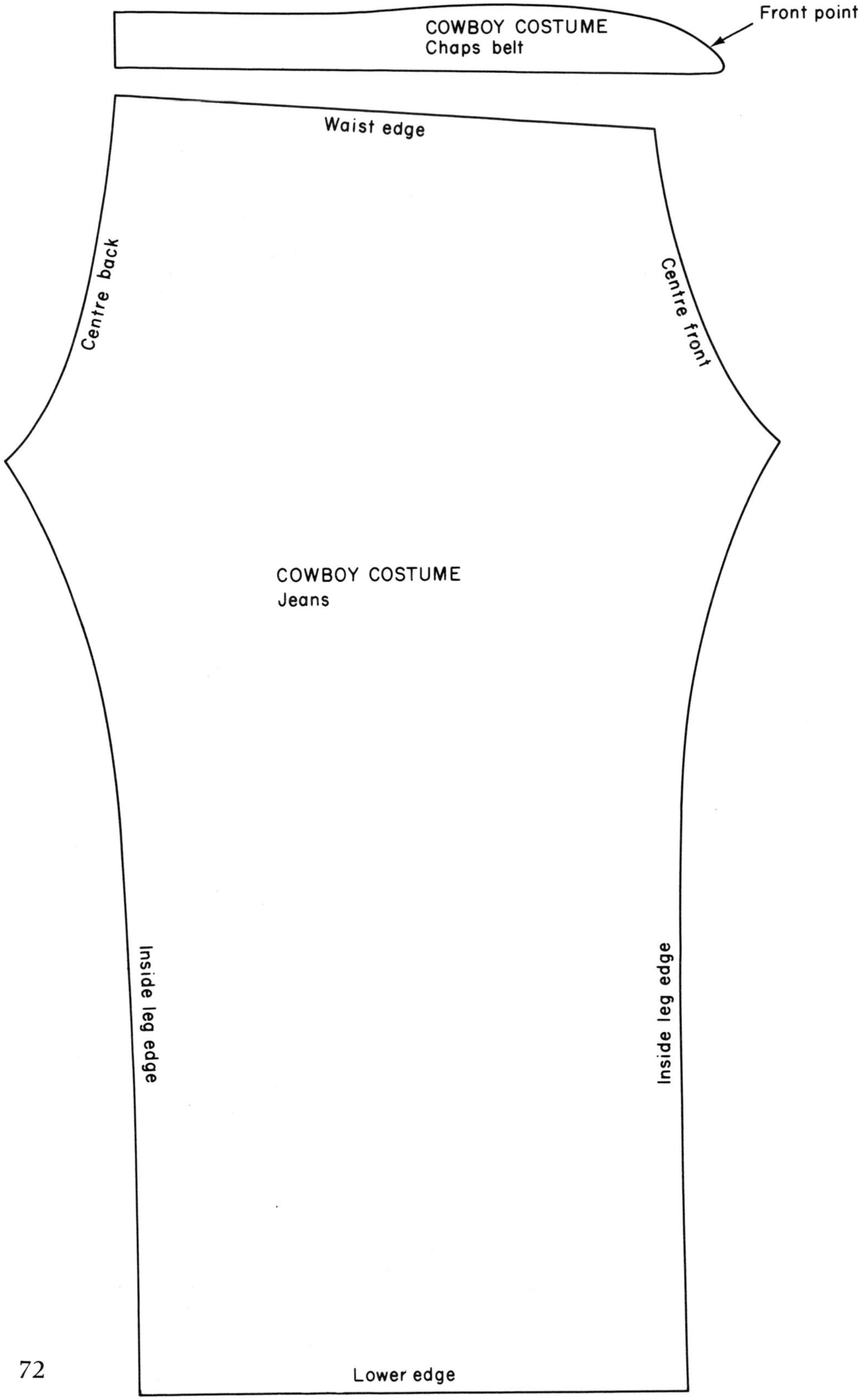

COWBOY COSTUME
Chaps belt

Front point

Waist edge

Centre back

Centre front

COWBOY COSTUME
Jeans

Inside leg edge

Inside leg edge

72

Lower edge

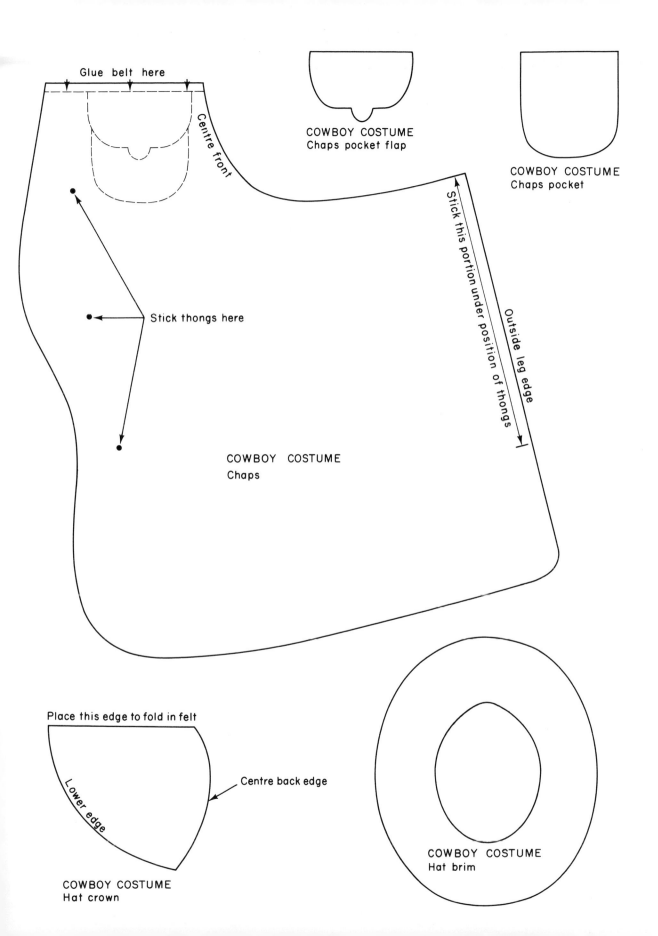

Glue belt here

Centre front

Stick thongs here

Stick this portion under position of thongs

Outside leg edge

COWBOY COSTUME
Chaps

COWBOY COSTUME
Chaps pocket flap

COWBOY COSTUME
Chaps pocket

Place this edge to fold in felt

Lower edge

Centre back edge

COWBOY COSTUME
Hat crown

COWBOY COSTUME
Hat brim

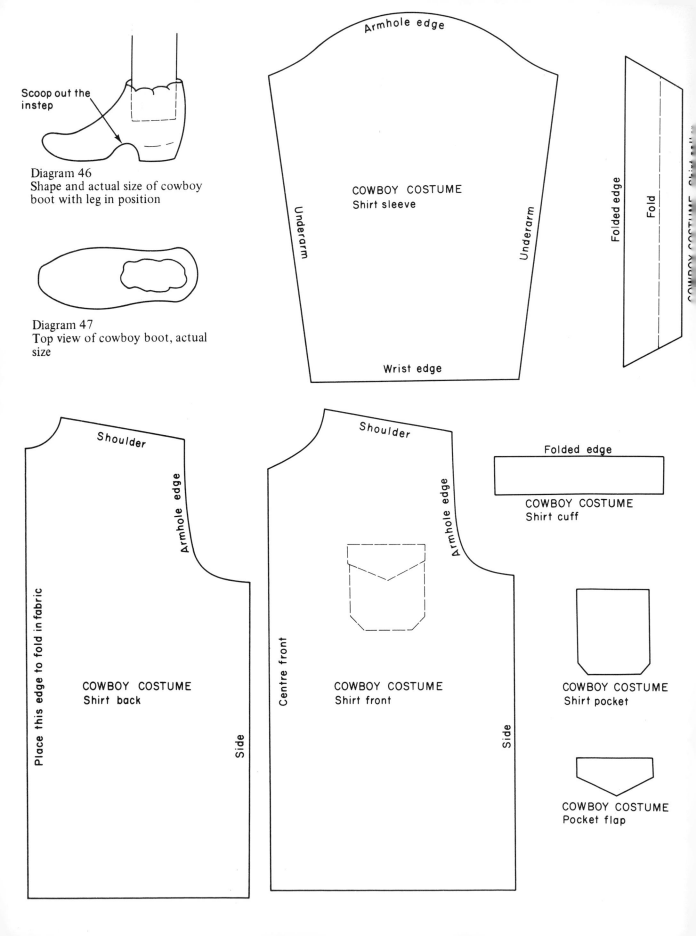

Scoop out the instep

Diagram 46
Shape and actual size of cowboy boot with leg in position

Diagram 47
Top view of cowboy boot, actual size

Armhole edge

COWBOY COSTUME
Shirt sleeve

Underarm

Underarm

Wrist edge

Folded edge

Fold

Shoulder

Armhole edge

Place this edge to fold in fabric

COWBOY COSTUME
Shirt back

Side

Shoulder

Armhole edge

Centre front

COWBOY COSTUME
Shirt front

Side

Folded edge

COWBOY COSTUME
Shirt cuff

COWBOY COSTUME
Shirt pocket

COWBOY COSTUME
Pocket flap

For the thongs cut six 6 cm ($2\frac{1}{4}$ in.) long very narrow strips of leather. Fold each in half and stick the folded ends at the positions shown on the chaps pattern. Just above the folded end of each thong stick on a small black bead. Now fold each chaps piece bringing the outside leg edge round until it is just underneath the line of thongs. Stick this edge in position as shown on the chaps pattern. Slip a chaps piece on each of the doll's legs and stick the right front point of the belt over the left front point. Stick on a bead at this position. Take the rest of the belt round the back of the doll and overlap and stick the ends, then make and stick on a buckle in the same way as for the jeans belt. Stick the cowboy boots in position on the ends of the doll's legs.

Hat

Use fawn or grey felt for this. Cut the hat brim from paper then stick this onto a piece of felt. Cut out the brim a tiny bit larger than the paper all round the outer edge then cut out the centre hole even with the paper. Stick the remaining side of the paper onto a piece of felt and cut out as before. Now press the brim with a hot iron and damp cloth to make it as thin as possible. While the brim is still damp, curl up the sides into the shape shown in the illustration. Place the brim in position on the doll's head, then spread a little glue round the head where the brim touches it to hold it in place.

Cut the crown of the hat from felt, placing the edge of the pattern indicated to a fold in the felt. Oversew the centre back edges together, then turn the crown right side out. Now stretch the top of the crown with the fingers to make it as rounded as possible. Run a gathering thread round the lower edge of the crown and place it on top of the brim of the hat pulling up the gathers to fit. Now stick the crown in this position, then push in the top as shown in the illustration. Stick a strip of narrow ribbon round for a hat band.

If desired, place a coil of rope in the cowboy's hands as shown in the illustration. Use thin string or cord for this and glue it in place.

German costume
Black Forest

The white straw hat, worn over a black cap with an eye veil, is decorated with large pompons. These are bright red for unmarried girls and black for married women. The bodice and the pleated skirt are black. The apron is made of green brocade fabric.

Doll

Make a basic female doll with legs and cover the hands and arms. Only a little hair is required around the face as the rest of the head is covered by the cap. Make the stockings from white stretchy fabric. Make the basic black stretchy nylon fabric shoes. To make the point on the upper part of each shoe, spread a little glue inside the shoe fabric, then pull the fabric towards the ankle using the point of a pin. Stick the pin into the foot to hold in place until the glue dries.

Underskirt

This should be made of red fabric. Cut a 14 cm by 36 cm (5½ in. by 14 in.) strip, turn in one long edge and stick to neaten, for the hem edge. Overlap and stick the short edges. Run a gathering thread round the remaining raw edge, put the underskirt on the doll, pull up the gathers round the waist and fasten off.

Skirt

Use thin soft black fabric for this because the skirt has to be pressed into pleats at the back. Cut a 15 cm by 46 cm (6 in. by 18 in.) strip. Turn in and stick one long edge for the hem. On the wrong side of the fabric and using a coloured pencil, draw lines at about 1 cm (⅜ in.) intervals as shown in diagram 48. Draw one line across the centre of the strip as shown in the diagram. Now take three running stitches through the lines as shown in the diagram. Pull up all three threads tightly and fasten off; this will evenly pleat the fabric. Press the pleats with a hot iron and a damp cloth, then remove the threads.

Overlap and stick the short edges of the skirt strip noting that this join will be at the centre front of the doll. Run a gathering thread round the raw waist edge, put the skirt on the doll, pull up the gathers round the waist and fasten off.

Apron

Use green or blue brocade fabric or plain dress lining fabric. Cut a 15 cm by 30 cm (6 in. by 12 in.) strip of fabric. Turn in and stick all the edges to neaten except for one 30 cm (12 in.) edge. Gather this edge to fit round the front waist of the doll, then stick this edge in place. Damp the fabric and arrange in folds then leave to dry.

Blouse

Use thin white cotton. For the blouse collar stick a bit of narrow blue and white braid round the doll's neck or alternatively a narrow strip of white fabric. Cut two sleeves from fabric, placing the edge of the pattern indicated to a fold each time. Keeping the fabric folded, join the underarm edges of each sleeve. Turn the sleeves right side out and run a gathering thread round the top edge. Put the sleeves on the doll, and pull up the gathers having them well up onto the shoulders. Fasten off the gathering threads. Run a gathering thread round each sleeve about 1 cm (⅜ in.) up from the folded edge. Pull up the gathers to fit the arms and fasten off.

Bodice

Make this from black felt. Cut out two bodice pieces then bring the edges of the darts together and over-sew as indicated on the pattern. Press one piece flat for the back of the bodice and coax the other piece into a rounded shape at the chest by stretching the felt with the fingers. Put both bodice pieces in position on the doll and oversew the shoulder edges together neatly. Bring the side edges together, and if necessary trim off any excess before oversewing, to make the bodice fit neatly to the shape of the doll. Oversew the waist edge of the bodice to the top raw edges of the skirt and apron. Stick narrow strips of braid or fabric with a small geometric pattern round the neck of the bodice and down each shoulder seam. Also stick braid across the front and back and over the shoulders at the armholes as shown by the dotted lines on the pattern.

Sash

Use a 56 cm (22 in.) length of 2.5 cm (1 in.) wide ribbon, to match the colour of the apron. Fringe out the ends then tie around the waist to cover the raw edges, making a bow at the back as shown in the illustration.

Eye veil

For this use thin stiff fabric such as organdie. Cut out the veil, then curl up the corners indicated on the pattern by rolling the fabric round a darning

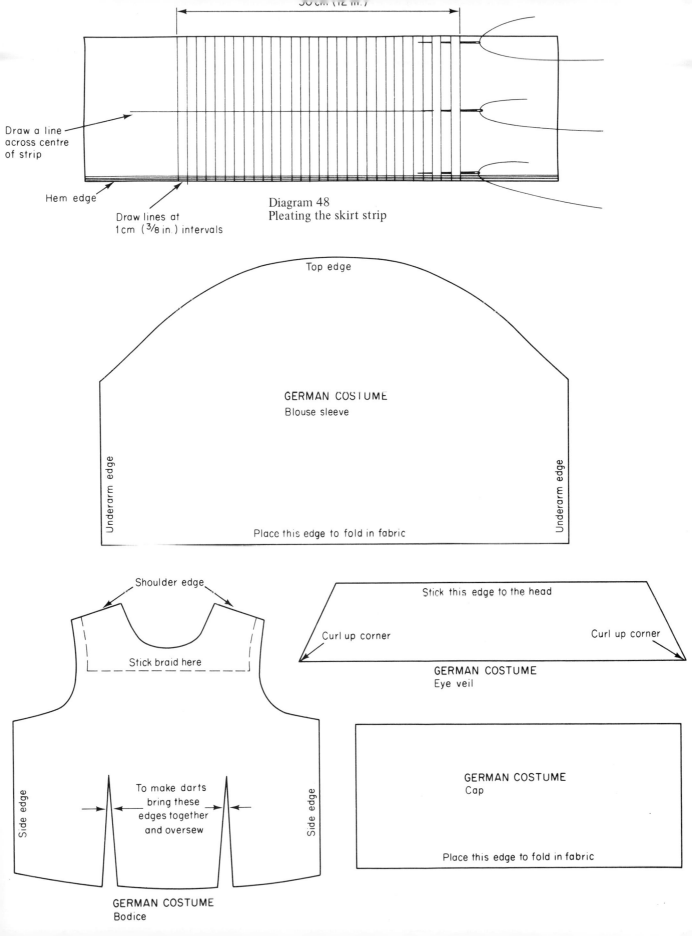

50 cm (12 in.)

Draw a line
across centre
of strip

Hem edge

Draw lines at
1 cm (³/₈ in.) intervals

Diagram 48
Pleating the skirt strip

Top edge

GERMAN COSTUME
Blouse sleeve

Underarm edge

Underarm edge

Place this edge to fold in fabric

Shoulder edge

Stick braid here

Side edge

Side edge

To make darts
bring these
edges together
and oversew

GERMAN COSTUME
Bodice

Stick this edge to the head

Curl up corner

Curl up corner

GERMAN COSTUME
Eye veil

GERMAN COSTUME
Cap

Place this edge to fold in fabric

needle. Stick the veil to the top of the head and down each side of the face as shown in the illustration.

Cap

Use black stretchy fabric for this, the same as used for the doll's shoes. First stick a length of very narrow ribbon to each side of the head for the cap ties and tie them in a bow under the doll's chin. Cut out the cap placing the edge indicated on the pattern to a fold in the fabric. Keeping the cap fabric folded join the short edges. Run a gathering thread round the remaining raw edges through both thicknesses, then pull up the gathers tightly and fasten off. Turn the cap right side out, put it on the doll's head lapping it over the veil, then stick in place.

Hat

This would be made of white straw and as a substitute, stiffened canvas interlining or any white fabric with a straw-like texture can be used. If the fabric is not stiff enough, a circle of firm paper should be glued between the layers when making the brim. For the crown of the hat use a bit of white stretchy fabric, for example a cutting off nylon tights or socks. The crown will be almost covered by the pompons.

Cut out two hat brim pieces. Cut a piece of the stretchy fabric about the size of the dotted circle shown on the hat brim pattern, then stick it onto one of the brim pieces to cover the centre hole. Now stick both hat pieces together sandwiching the stretchy fabric piece between them. Before the glue dries, place the hat on the doll's head and bend the brim down at the front and back as illustrated. Remove the hat and spread the centre stretchy piece with glue. Place the hat on the doll's head pulling the brim down to stretch the centre fabric circle. Hold the hat in place with pins until the glue is dry.

The red woollen pompons can be made from a variety of fabrics. Thin velvet is best because the pile on the velvet looks like wool tufts. Towelling, close-pile fur fabric or felt can also be used if velvet is not available.

Cut seven large and four small pompons using the patterns. Run a gathering thread round the edge of each one, put a little stuffing in the centre then pull up the gathers tightly and fasten off. Stick the pompons on the hat as shown in diagram 49, grouping the seven large ones together tightly to cover the crown of the hat. The four small ones should be stuck to the back of the hat brim.

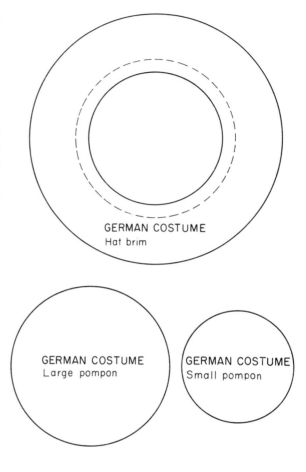

GERMAN COSTUME
Hat brim

GERMAN COSTUME
Large pompon

GERMAN COSTUME
Small pompon

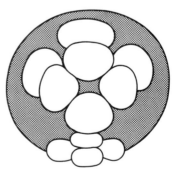

Diagram 49
The pompons stuck on the hat brim, with four small pompons at the back

80

Scottish fishwife costume
Newhaven and Fisherrow

82

The underskirt and overskirt are made from striped fabric. The underskirt is blue and white, and the overskirt dark and light blue lined with stripes of red and white. The blouse of floral material has white cuffs and the head scarf and shawl can be checked or plain. The creel fish basket is very easy to make from ordinary paper drinking straws, and it contains herring made from modelling clay.

Doll

Make a basic female doll with legs and cover the hands and arms. When sticking the leg tubes inside the body cone, tilt the cone at the angle shown in diagram 50. This pose will help to balance the creel of fish on the finished doll. Only a little hair is required at the front of the doll's head as the remainder is covered by the scarf. Use black stretchy fabric for the stockings. Make the basic black stretchy nylon shoes and oversew the top edges at the fronts together almost as far as the ankle, then stick on small bows of thick thread for laces.

Petticoat

Use any oddment of plain fabric. Cut a 14 cm by 36 cm (5½ in. by 14 in.) strip. Turn in and stick one long edge to neaten. Overlap and stick the short edges then gather the remaining raw edge and put the skirt on the doll. Pull up the gathers round the waist and fasten off.

Underskirt

Use blue and white striped fabric. Cut a 15 cm by 40 cm (6 in. by 16 in.) strip then make in the same way as for the petticoat.

Blouse

Use flower-patterned fabric for the blouse and plain white fabric for the cuffs. Cut out the blouse placing the edge indicated on the pattern to a fold in the fabric. Cut the blouse open down the centre front, then turn in the right front edge and stick down, to neaten. Cut two blouse cuff pieces, placing the edge of the pattern indicated to a fold in the fabric each time. Keeping the cuff pieces folded, join the long raw edges to the elbow edges of the blouse having the wrong sides of the fabric together so that the raw edges of the seam will be on the right side of the blouse.

Now join the underarm and side edges of the blouse as far as the cuff seams. Turn the blouse right

side out then join the raw edges of the cuffs. Turn the cuffs back up over the sleeves. Put the blouse on the doll and stick the right front edge over the left front edge. Stick small beads down the centre front for buttons.

Overskirt

If dark and light blue striped fabric is not available for the overskirt, a piece of blue and white striped fabric (as used for the underskirt) can be dyed blue to produce dark and light stripes. The skirt lining is red and white striped fabric.

Cut a 15 cm by 50 cm (6 in. by 20 in.) strip of each fabric. Join the pieces together along one long edge taking a tiny seam. Bring the short edges of the strips together and join them also. Turn right side out and bring the remaining raw edges of each strip together then press the hem edge of the skirt. Run a gathering thread round the raw edges through both thicknesses, put the skirt on the doll, pull up the gathers round the waist and fasten off.

Cut the waistband from dark and light blue striped fabric. Turn in the long edges and stick, to neaten. Glue the waistband round the top edge of the skirt to cover the raw edges, trimming off any excess length and overlapping and sticking the short edges at the centre back. Tie a length of thin cord round the overskirt just below the waistband making a small bow at the front. Now lift the overskirt at each side and tuck the hem into the cord. Use dabs of glue to hold it in place and arrange the overskirt in folds exactly as shown in the illustrations.

Headscarf

Cut an 11 cm (4¼ in.) square of checked or plain fabric. Fray out the raw edges a little to form a fringe then fold, corner to corner, and put the scarf on the doll's head. Tuck and stick the corners under the chin.

Shawl

Cut a 14 cm (5½ in.) square of checked or plain fabric and fray out the edges to form fringe. Damp the shawl then fold corner to corner and place around the doll's shoulders. Knot the shawl at the front and when the fabric is dry, stick the knot in place.

Creel

About twenty paper drinking straws are required for this. First flatten each straw slightly by pulling it

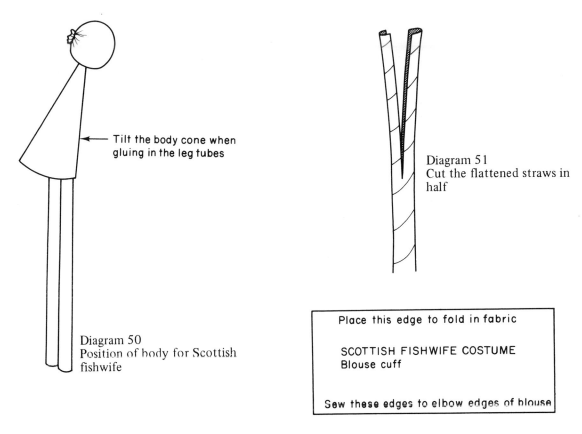

Tilt the body cone when
gluing in the leg tubes

Diagram 50
Position of body for Scottish
fishwife

Diagram 51
Cut the flattened straws in
half

Place this edge to fold in fabric

SCOTTISH FISHWIFE COSTUME
Blouse cuff

Sew these edges to elbow edges of blouse

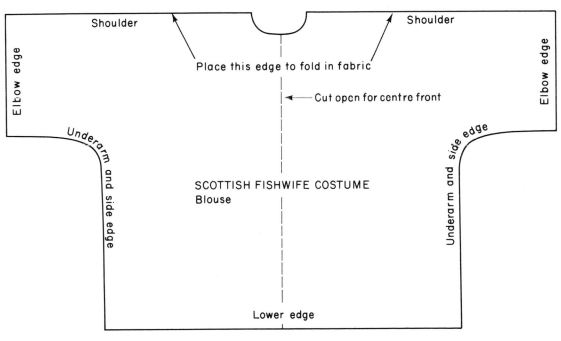

Shoulder   Shoulder

Place this edge to fold in fabric

Cut open for centre front

Elbow edge

Elbow edge

Underarm and side edge

Underarm and side edge

SCOTTISH FISHWIFE COSTUME
Blouse

Lower edge

SCOTTISH FISHWIFE COSTUME
Overskirt waistband

between the finger and thumb then cut each one in half along the length as shown in diagram 51. Trace the creel pattern off the page onto thin paper and mark on all the lines. Cut out the pattern and stick it centrally on a 25 cm (10 in.) square of card. Now place 13 cm (5 in.) lengths of straw on the pattern at the positions of the lines sticking the lower ends of the straws to the card below the lower edge of the pattern. When all the straws are in position place a strip of sticky tape over them at the lower ends to hold them securely in place as shown in diagram 52. Now using the remaining straws, weave them in and out of the straws on the card as shown in the diagram. As each straw is woven in, stick them to the vertical straws at each end to hold them in place.

When the paper pattern is completely covered by the straws, lift off the sticky tape at the lower edge and remove the woven piece carefully off the card. Trim the top ends off the vertical straws leaving about 5 mm ($\frac{1}{4}$ in.), then turn over and stick these ends to the wrong side of the woven piece. Trim off the ends of the horizontal straws at each side even with the vertical straws, then bring these side edges together and overlap and stick neatly. Cut the creel base from card using the pattern. Place it inside the lower edge of the creel then bend and stick the lower ends of the vertical straws onto it. To make a neat finish along the top edge of the creel, take a straw and twist it all along the length then flatten the twists. Stick this strip round the top of the creel. The creel can now be painted with brown water colour, or enamel paint diluted with turpentine.

For the carrying strap cut a 22 cm (8$\frac{1}{2}$ in.) long narrow strip of leather, or use narrow braid or shoe lace. Thread the strap through the creel at each side about three woven straws down from the top. Knot the ends of the strap on the inside. Place the creel in position on the doll with the strap passing around the forehead, then adjust the length of the strap if necessary to fit as shown in the illustrations.

To make the herring, roll out small tapered sausage shapes from modelling clay, to the size shown in diagram 53. Cut out and shape the tail with a pen-knife and make small indentations for the fins, mouth and eye. When the clay has hardened, colour the fish with silvery paint underneath and bluish-green on top.

The creel can be packed with crumpled tissue paper and then only a few fish need to be made and glued on top of the paper. Finally, fit the creel on the doll and stick the strap to the forehead.

The stand
Because the creel makes this doll rather top heavy it is glued on to a simple stand made from a piece of cork. The cork is about 13 mm ($\frac{1}{2}$ in.) thick and measures 8 cm by 10 cm (3 in. by 4 in.). Sandpaper the top edges to chamfer them, then place the doll's feet in position on the stand. Mark the positions of the feet on the cork by drawing round them with a pencil. Now spread glue liberally on these marked positions and also on the soles of the doll's feet. When the glue is tacky, position the doll on the stand again and stick several pins through each foot and into the cork. Remove the pins when the glue is quite dry.

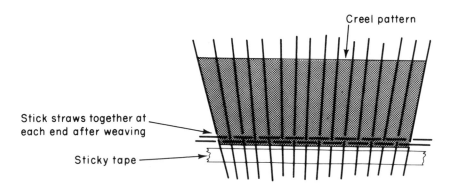

Diagram 52
Weaving the creel basket

86

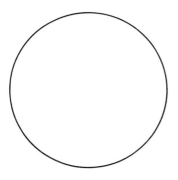

SCOTTISH FISHWIFE COSTUME
Creel base

Diagram 53
Shape of herring

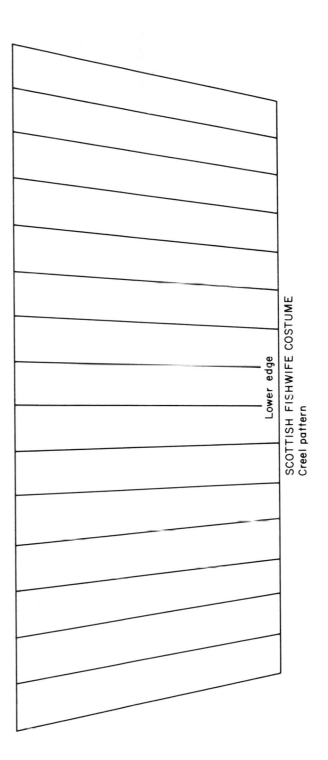

Lower edge

SCOTTISH FISHWIFE COSTUME
Creel pattern

London pearly queen costume

The pearlies' costumes are decorated with thousands of real pearl buttons sewn on to make the most beautiful and elaborate patterns. For the dolls illustrated, lengths of white plastic pearl sequins sold by the metre or yard are used. The woman wears a wide-brimmed hat covered with coloured ostrich feathers and decorated with sparkling brooches. Black felt is the best material to use for both the pearly costumes and all edges should be joined by oversewing them together. The sequin lengths should first be spread with a preliminary coating of glue before finally sticking in position, to make them adhere properly. When sequins have to be stuck around a curve, for example a sleeve edge, they can be bent with small pliers to fit the curve.

Doll

Make a basic female doll with legs and cover the hands and neck. For the hair use crêpe hair or embroidery thread making a centre parting and gathering the hair to the back of the neck. For the stockings use flesh or tan nylon stocking fabric.

Make the basic black stretchy nylon shoes then cut two small 'tongues' from black felt and stick one to the front of each shoe.

Thread tiny pearl or white beads and fix round the neck for necklaces. For each earring thread a few beads and stick to each side of the face below the hair.

Scarf

Cut a 10 cm (4 in.) square of thin red nylon or silky fabric. Fold it corner to corner and stick around the doll's neck knotting it at the centre front.

Skirt

Note that about 5 m (5½ yd) of sequins are required for the woman's costume. Cut out the skirt placing the edge of the pattern indicated to a fold in the felt. Run a gathering thread round the waist edge then put the skirt around the doll, pull up the gathers to fit the waist and fasten off the thread. Take the skirt off the doll and stick on lengths of sequins as shown by the dotted lines on the pattern. To do this easily, first spread about 2 cm (1 in.) of the back of the sequins with glue and stick in position, then continue about 2 cm (1 in.) at a time gluing and pressing the length in place. Now stick on circles of sequins and the curved lines as shown in the illustrations.

When all the sequins are fixed in place, put the skirt on the doll and overlap and stick the centre back edges at the centre back of the doll.

Jacket

To make the full-sized jacket pattern, fold a piece of thin paper, place the fold to the edge indicated on the pattern then trace it. Cut out and open up the pattern. Cut out the jacket placing the edge of the pattern indicated to a fold in the felt. Cut the jacket open at the centre front then cut the fronts at the neck and lower edges as shown by the dotted lines on the pattern.

Join the underarm and side edges then turn right side out and press. Now stick sequins to the jacket as shown in the illustrations, to match the skirt. Put the jacket on the doll and stick the front edges together edge to edge. Cut the collar from felt and stick on two rows of sequins, then stick the collar round the neck of the jacket.

Hat

Cut the hat brim from felt and stick sequins all round the edge. Place the brim on the doll's head as shown

90

in the illustration and stick in place. The top of the head will be covered by the feathers. On the doll illustrated the feathers are bits of swansdown and marabou dress trimmings. These can be gently curled by pulling the feathers gently but firmly between the thumb and a blunt knife blade. Stick feathers all over the top of the hat having them curling from the front of the hat towards the back. For the sparkling brooches stick bits of junk jewellery to the front of the hat, underneath the brim and also to the neck scarf. Diamante clasp fastenings off old necklaces make excellent brooches.

LONDON PEARLY COSTUME
(WOMAN)
Hat brim

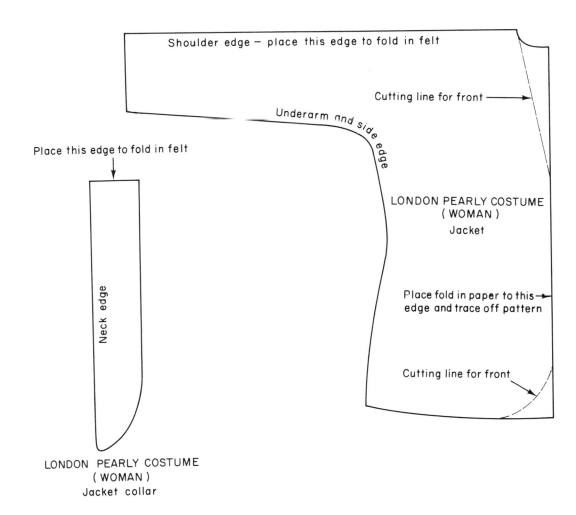

Shoulder edge — place this edge to fold in felt

Cutting line for front ⟶

Underarm and side edge

LONDON PEARLY COSTUME
(WOMAN)
Jacket

Place fold in paper to this ⟶
edge and trace off pattern

Cutting line for front

Place this edge to fold in felt

Neck edge

LONDON PEARLY COSTUME
(WOMAN)
Jacket collar

91

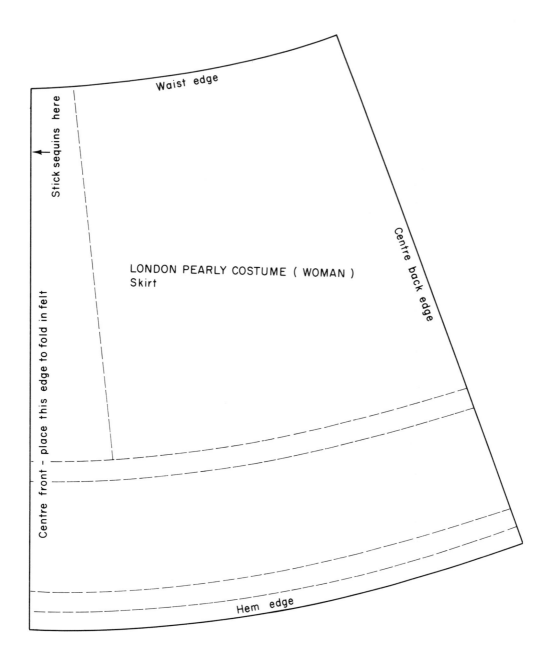

Waist edge

Stick sequins here

Centre back edge

LONDON PEARLY COSTUME (WOMAN)
Skirt

Centre front - place this edge to fold in felt

Hem edge

92

London pearly king costume

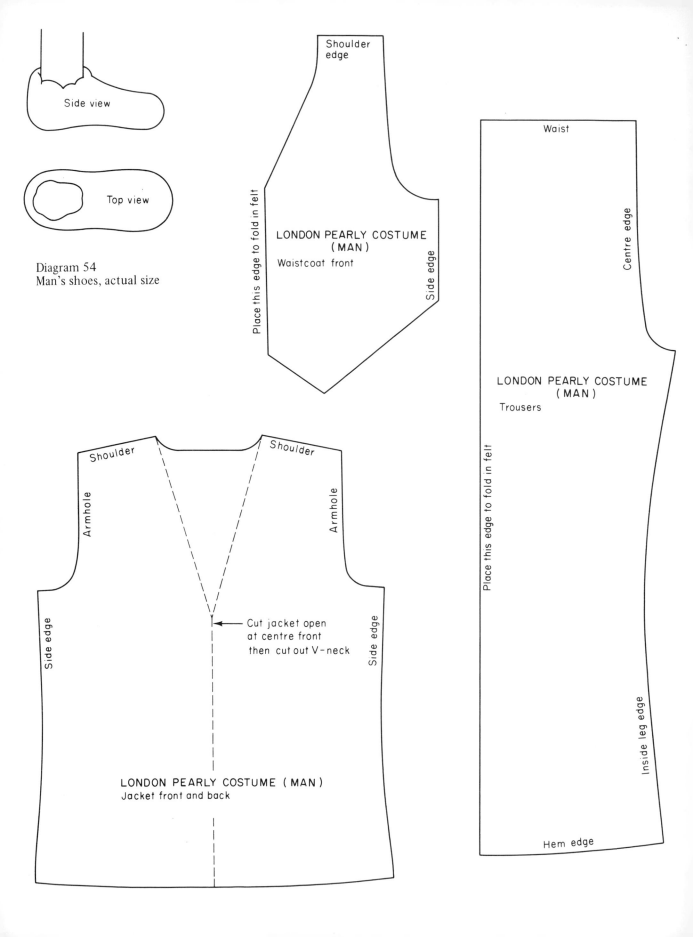

Side view

Top view

Diagram 54
Man's shoes, actual size

Shoulder edge

Place this edge to fold in felt

LONDON PEARLY COSTUME
(MAN)
Waistcoat front

Side edge

Waist

Centre edge

LONDON PEARLY COSTUME
(MAN)

Trousers

Place this edge to fold in felt

Inside leg edge

Hem edge

Shoulder

Shoulder

Armhole

Armhole

Side edge

Side edge

Cut jacket open
at centre front
then cut out V-neck

LONDON PEARLY COSTUME (MAN)
Jacket front and back

The man wears a button-decorated suit, the waist-coat of which is entirely covered with buttons. Like the woman, he wears a scarf knotted around the neck.

Doll

Make a basic male doll and cover the hands. The shoes are made from modelling clay as given in the basic doll instructions, then painted black. Diagram 54 shows the actual size of the shoes. Do not stick them in place on the legs until the trousers are in position on the doll.

Shirt front

Cut a 4 cm (1½ in.) square of white cotton fabric and stick it to the chest just below the chin. Stick a few tiny beads down the centre for buttons.

Scarf

Cut a 10 cm (4 in.) square of thin red nylon or silky fabric. Fold, corner to corner, and knot round the doll's neck as shown in the illustration. Stick the ends to each side so that they will be tucked inside the V-neck of the waistcoat when it is glued in place later on.

Trousers

Note that about 6 m (6½ yd) of sequins are required for the man's costume. Cut two trouser pieces, placing the edge indicated on the pattern to a fold in the felt each time. Join the trouser pieces to each other at the centre edges. Bring the inside leg edges of each leg together and oversew. Turn the trousers right side out and press the seams. Stretch the felt at the hem edge of the trouser legs to make them flare out slightly. Now stick two rows of sequins round the hem edge of each trouser leg and a row up the leg at each side. Finally stick on sequins in patterns as shown in the illustrations.

Put the trousers on the doll and, if necessary, push a little stuffing in the seat of the trousers to shape them. Run a gathering thread round the waist edge, pull up the gathers and fasten off. Now stick the shoes in place.

Waistcoat

Only the waistcoat front needs to be made. Cut out the waistcoat front placing the edge indicated on the pattern to a fold in the felt. Stick rows of sequins to the waistcoat front to cover it completely. Stick the waistcoat to the doll at the side and shoulder edges.

Jacket

Cut two jacket pieces from felt. Cut one piece open at the centre front for the jacket fronts, then cut out the V-neck shape as shown on the pattern. Join the fronts to the back at the shoulder and side edges.

Cut two sleeves from felt and join the underarm seams of each one. Turn the sleeves right side out. Now oversew the armhole edge of each sleeve to the armholes of the jacket as shown in diagram 55 having the right sides together. Turn the jacket right side out and stick on sequins as shown in the illustrations. Put the jacket on the doll. Cut the collar from felt placing the edge indicated on the pattern to a fold in the felt. Stick on sequins to cover the collar then stick it round the neck edge of the jacket.

Cap

First cut a 1 cm (⅜ in.) wide strip of felt, long enough to go around the doll's head, for the cap band. Stick the band in place across the doll's forehead at the front and tilted slightly lower at one side of the head than the other.

Cut two cap crown pieces from felt, and cut the centre hole out of one piece as shown by the dotted line on the pattern. Join the crown pieces together round the outer edges. Turn right side out and press. Now place the crown of the cap on the doll's head lapping the inner edge about 5 mm (¼ in.) over the cap band. Slip stitch this edge to the cap band all round. Tilt the crown of the cap to one side and catch to the doll's head with a stitch.

Stick on sequins to completely cover the top of the cap. Cut the cap peak from felt and stick on a row of sequins. Now thread tiny pearl or white beads and stick them along the outer edge of the cap peak. Spread the inner edge of the peak with glue, and stick it just beneath the cap band at the centre front as illustrated. Now stick two more rows of threaded beads to the band above the cap peak.

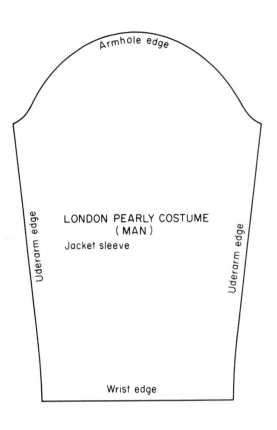

Armhole edge

Uderarm edge

LONDON PEARLY COSTUME
(MAN)

Jacket sleeve

Uderarm edge

Wrist edge

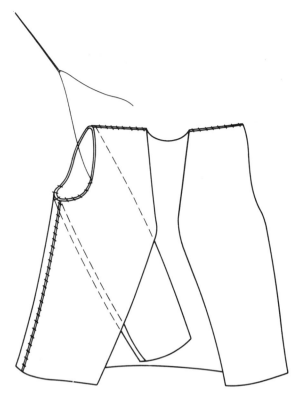

Diagram 55
How to sew the sleeves to the jacket
armholes

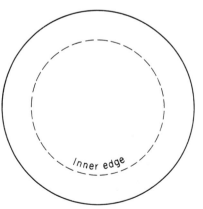

Inner edge

LONDON PEARLY COSTUME (MAN)
Crown of cap

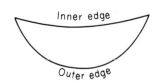

Inner edge

Outer edge

LONDON PEARLY COSTUME (MAN)
Cap peak

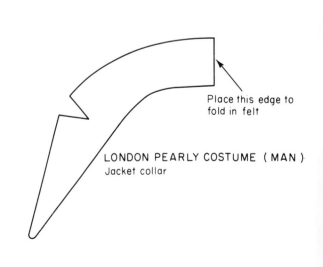

Place this edge to
fold in felt

LONDON PEARLY COSTUME (MAN)
Jacket collar

Netherlands mother
costume
Volendam

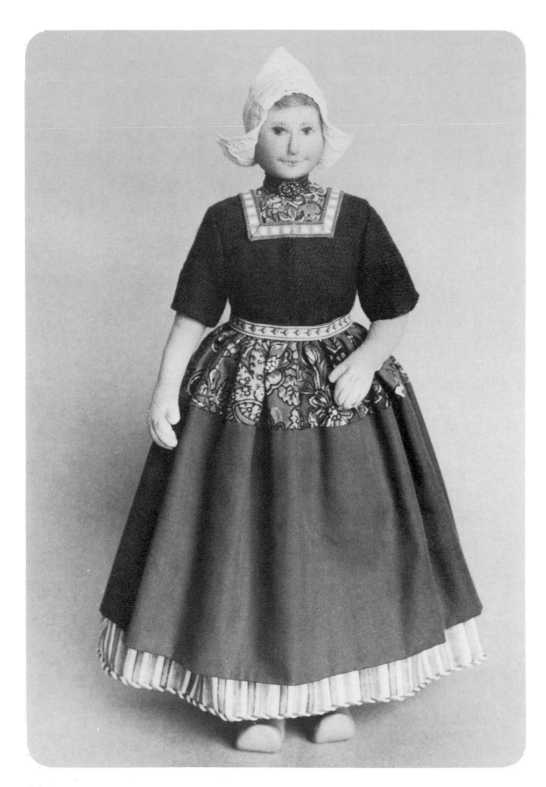

98

The mother wears a 'seven coloured' striped skirt and over this a dark blue blouse. The blue apron has a strip of floral fabric across the top which matches the fabric at the neck of the blouse. A white lacy cap covers the hair and a necklace of coral beads is worn around the neck. The wooden clogs are made from modelling clay.

Doll

Make a basic female doll with legs and cover the hands, arms and neck. Stick a little fair hair to the forehead and the back of the neck, the remainder of the head will be covered by the cap. Do not make pipe cleaner feet on this doll because the leg tubes will be stuck into the modelled clogs.

Stockings

Use dark blue stretchy fabric for these, such as cuttings off old socks, stockings or a thin sweater. Pin the stocking pattern onto a folded piece of the fabric, placing the edge of the pattern indicated to the fold. Trim the fabric even with the pattern at the upper and lower edges then stitch close to the pattern at the edge marked 'stitching line'. Remove the pattern and trim off the fabric close to the stitching line. Turn the stockings right side out and put them on the doll's legs, sticking the lower edges securely to the lower edges of the leg tubes, and the upper edges to the legs.

Clogs

Roll two equal sized balls of modelling clay, making them about 2.5 cm (1 in.) in diameter. Roll each into an egg shape and flatten slightly, then flatten the narrow ends a little more for the back parts of the clogs. Now tip up each clog at the front end, rolling against a flat surface to turn up to a point. Shape the point a little more then push the leg tubes into the back part of the clogs. Take the clogs carefully off the leg tubes and scoop out the excess clay. Now continue shaping the clogs as shown in the actual size drawings in diagram 56. Put them aside to harden, then rub with sandpaper to improve the shape if necessary. Finally paint the clogs a creamy yellow colour. The leg tubes can be glued inside the clogs at this stage, and if so the doll should be put aside until the glue is quite dry. Alternatively, they can be glued in place after dressing the doll.

Underskirts

Two of these are required, the first one dark blue, and the second blue and white striped fabric. Both skirts are made in the same way. Cut a 15 cm by 40 cm (6 in. by 15½ in.) strip of fabric. Turn in and stick one long edge to neaten for the hem, then overlap and stick the short edges. Run a gathering thread round the remaining raw edge, put the skirt on the doll then pull up the gathers round the waist and fasten off.

Seven-coloured skirt

This has stripes of red, dark blue, light blue, yellow, green, white and black and it would be almost impossible to find suitable fabric striped in these colours except perhaps in Holland. However a piece of fabric can be coloured with marker pens by ruling the lines onto the fabric. For the skirt on the doll illustrated, a piece of white fabric which has very thin black stripes at about 5 mm (¼ in.) intervals is used. The stripes act as guide lines when ruling the coloured stripes, but plain white fabric can be ruled with a pen or pencil at regular intervals to get the same effect. Diagram 57 shows an enlarged pattern of stripes of varying widths using all the colours, but any other combinations can be devised.

A 16 cm by 46 cm (6¼ in. by 18 in.) strip is required for the skirt, but cut a piece of fabric slightly larger all round than this, then cut to size after ruling the stripes. Pin the fabric to a piece of board then rule on the stripes. When the piece is quite dry cut out the skirt then make up and fix in position on the doll in the same way as for the underskirt. *Do not* wet this skirt to make it drape properly because the colours may run.

For the red and white twisted cord around the hem of the skirt use thick thread. Cut a 140 cm (55 in.) length of white thread and also of red thread. Fold the lengths in half and knot all the ends together. Catch the knotted ends round something to anchor them, then, keeping the threads taut, twist the other folded ends by rolling them between the fingers until the thread begins to curl up when it is slackened. Continue twisting then fold in half along the thread to curl up tightly. Stick the cord to the hem edge of the skirt all round.

Neck piece

Use multi-coloured flower printed fabric for this, and note that a piece of the same fabric is also used for

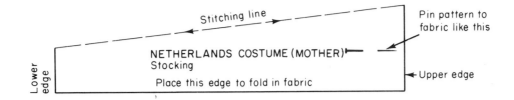

Stitching line

Pin pattern to
fabric like this

NETHERLANDS COSTUME (MOTHER)
Stocking

Lower
edge

Place this edge to fold in fabric

← Upper edge

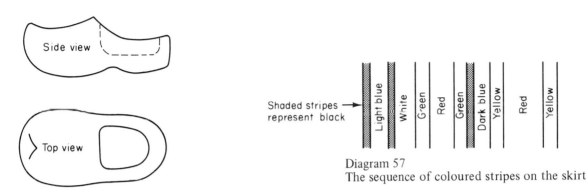

Side view

Top view

Diagram 56
Mother's clog, actual size

Shaded stripes → represent black

Light blue | White | Green | Red | Green | Dark blue | Yellow | Red | Yellow

Diagram 57
The sequence of coloured stripes on the skirt

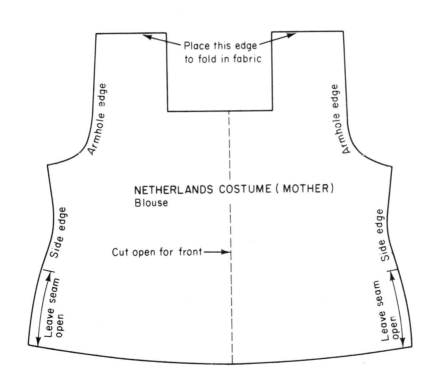

Place this edge
to fold in fabric

Armhole edge

Armhole edge

NETHERLANDS COSTUME (MOTHER)
Blouse

Side edge

Side edge

Cut open for front →

Leave seam open

Leave seam open

the top of the apron. Cut out two neck pieces, then on the front piece cut out the neck edge to the shape shown on the pattern. Stick the back piece in position on the doll, then stick on the front piece, lapping the shoulder edges over the back piece.

Necklace

Use tiny red beads for this. Thread three strands to fit closely round the doll's neck leaving a small gap at the front of the neck for the clasp. Use a short length of thin gold cord or thread, coiled into shape as illustrated, for the clasp, then stick in place.

Blouse

Use dark blue fabric or felt. Cut out the blouse, placing the edge indicated on the pattern to a fold in the fabric. Cut the blouse open at the front along the dotted line indicated. Turn in and stick the right front edge and the lower edges to neaten. Cut out two sleeves then turn in and stick the elbow edges to neaten. Place the armhole edges of the sleeves and blouse together and stitch in place. Now join the side and underarm edges leaving the lower part of the side seams open as shown on the pattern. Turn in the remaining raw edges of the side seams and stick down, to neaten. Put the blouse on the doll, lap the right front over the left front and stick in place.

Narrow blue and white braid is required for trimming the neck of the blouse. Alternatively, narrow pieces can be cut off suitably striped fabric, turning in and sticking the raw edges to neaten. The blouse illustrated is trimmed in this way and the apron waistband is also cut from the same piece of fabric. Stick the fabric strips or braid around the neck of the blouse to cover the raw edges.

Apron

Cut a 35 cm by 10 cm (14 in. by 4 in.) strip of blue fabric and a 35 cm by 4 cm (14 in. by 1½ in.) strip of flower printed fabric. Join the fabrics along one long edge. Turn in and stick the remaining raw edges to neaten except for the long edge of the printed fabric. Gather this edge to measure 10 cm (4 in.). Stick the gathered edge to the doll's waist then glue a strip of braid or fabric round for the waistband to cover the raw edges, overlapping and sticking the ends at the back.

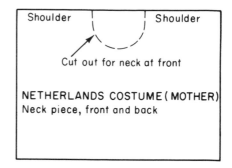

NETHERLANDS COSTUME (MOTHER)
Neck piece, front and back

NETHERLANDS COSTUME (MOTHER)
Blouse sleeve

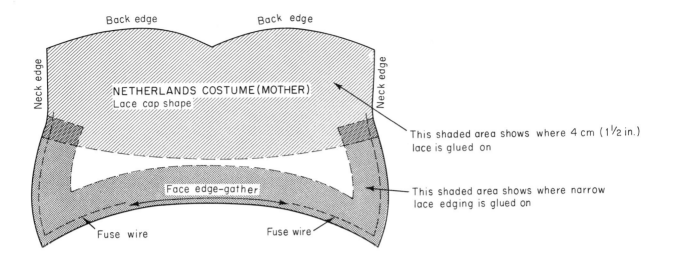

Back edge   Back edge

Neck edge

NETHERLANDS COSTUME (MOTHER)
Lace cap shape

Neck edge

This shaded area shows where 4 cm (1½ in.) lace is glued on

This shaded area shows where narrow lace edging is glued on

Face edge-gather

Fuse wire   Fuse wire

Lace cap

First of all cut a foundation shape from thin net fabric, muslin, or plain lace using the pattern. To stiffen the side 'wings', thread a needle with thinnest fuse wire and work running stitches at each side of the foundation shape as shown on the pattern. Now stick narrow lace edging to each surface of the foundation shape around the face edge and the wings, then stick on a piece of wider lace to cover the back part of the cap, as shown by the shaded areas on the pattern.

Now fold the cap in half bringing the wings together and join the back edges. Leaving the cap inside out, gather the neck edge and pull up the gathers to fit the back of the doll's neck. Run a gathering thread at the face edge as shown on the pattern, pull up the gathers a little and fasten off. Turn the cap right side out, glue it to the doll's head, then turn up the wings at each side as shown in the illustration.

Netherlands fisherman costume
Volendam

The father's baggy trousers, astrakhan cap and scarf are black. The jacket is red and white striped fabric with black buttons.

The doll

Make a basic male doll and cover the hands. Stick on fair hair around the sides and back of the head. This doll is in a seated position and if this pose is desired the leg tubes must be bent to shape as shown in diagram 58. After wrapping the stuffing around the doll, secure the legs in the bent position by sewing the body stuffing to the tops of the legs and catching the stuffing with stitches at the backs of the knees. The doll illustrated sits on an upturned fish basket, which can be made in the same way as the Scottish fishwife's creel, making it a little wider and not quite so deep.

Clogs

Make these in the same way as for the mother's clogs, but a little larger as shown in the actual size diagram 59. Take care to push the leg tubes into the clogs while the doll is in the seated position so that they will fit properly on the finished doll.

Scarf

Using black silky fabric cut a 12 cm (4¾ in.) square. Fold it corner to corner and place around the doll's neck lapping one corner over the other at the front. Stick these corners to the body.

Jacket

This should be made from finely striped red and white fabric. A good substitute to use is any white fabric with a ribbed weave, for example cotton needlecord. If the surface of the fabric is rubbed over with a red marker pen, only the ribs will be coloured thus giving a red and white striped effect. When cutting out the jacket pieces, take care to have the stripes running in the direction shown on the patterns.

Cut out the jacket placing the edge indicated on the pattern to a fold in the fabric. Turn in the back and front neck edges and the front edges and stick down to neaten. Join the front shoulder edges to the back shoulder edges.

Cut two sleeve pieces and join the underarm edges of each piece. Turn the sleeves right side out and join the armhole edges to the armhole edges of the jacket placing the underarm sleeve seams at point A on the jacket. Turn the jacket right side out and either stick or sew small black beads for buttons at the positions indicated by the dots on the pattern, that is, eight on the left front edge and one on each shoulder seam. Put the jacket on the doll and overlap and stick the front edges as illustrated. Gather the wrist edge of each sleeve a little and fasten off. Cut two jacket wrist band pieces, then turn in and stick the long edges to neaten. Stick a band round the wrist edge of each sleeve to cover the raw edges.

Trousers

Use plain black cotton or woollen fabric. Cut out two trouser pieces and join them at the centre front and back edges. Bring these seams together and join the inside leg edges of each leg. Run a gathering thread round the waist edge and put the trousers on the doll. If necessary push a little stuffing down the back of the trousers to shape the seat then pull up the gathers round the waist and fasten off. Run a gathering thread round each ankle edge of the trousers then pull up the gathers slightly and fasten off. Turn the gathered ankle edges to the inside so that the trousers pouch over at the lower edges as shown in the illustration.

Cut out the trouser waistband, turn in and stick the long edges to neaten, then glue the band round the waist edge of the trousers, overlapping and sticking the short edges at the centre back, and trimming off any excess length if necessary.

For the large silver buttons on the waistband at the front, use silver bits taken off pieces of junk jewellery, or small circles of card can be painted silver. Now glue the leg tubes into the clogs.

Hat

This can be made from any woven or knitted material which resembles astrakhan. The cap illustrated is made from a piece of towelling dyed black with a marker pen.

Cut out the hat side piece then turn in one long edge and stick to neaten. Join the short edges. Cut the hat top piece and place it inside the top raw edge of the side piece. Sew the edges together all round. Turn the hat right side out and stick it on the doll's head as illustrated.

Fishing net

This is simply a brown hair net, the thicker type used for sleeping in. Remove the elastic round the edge and then drape the net over the doll's hands.

NETHERLANDS COSTUME (FATHER)
Hat, side piece

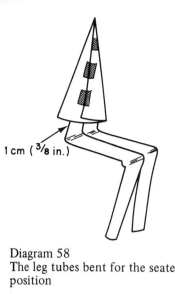

1 cm (³⁄₈ in.)

Diagram 58
The leg tubes bent for the seated
position

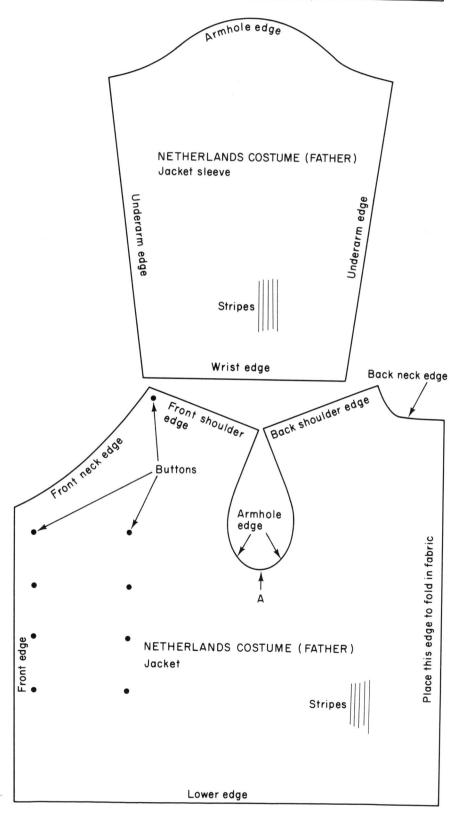

Armhole edge

NETHERLANDS COSTUME (FATHER)
Jacket sleeve

Underarm edge

Underarm edge

Stripes

Wrist edge

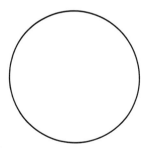

Side view

Top view

Diagram 59
Father's clog, actual size

Front shoulder
edge

Back neck edge

Back shoulder edge

Front neck edge

Buttons

Armhole
edge

A

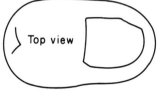

Place this edge to fold in fabric

NETHERLANDS COSTUME (FATHER)
Hat, top piece

Front edge

NETHERLANDS COSTUME (FATHER)
Jacket

Stripes

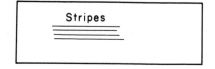

Stripes

NETHERLANDS COSTUME (FATHER)
Jacket wristband

Lower edge

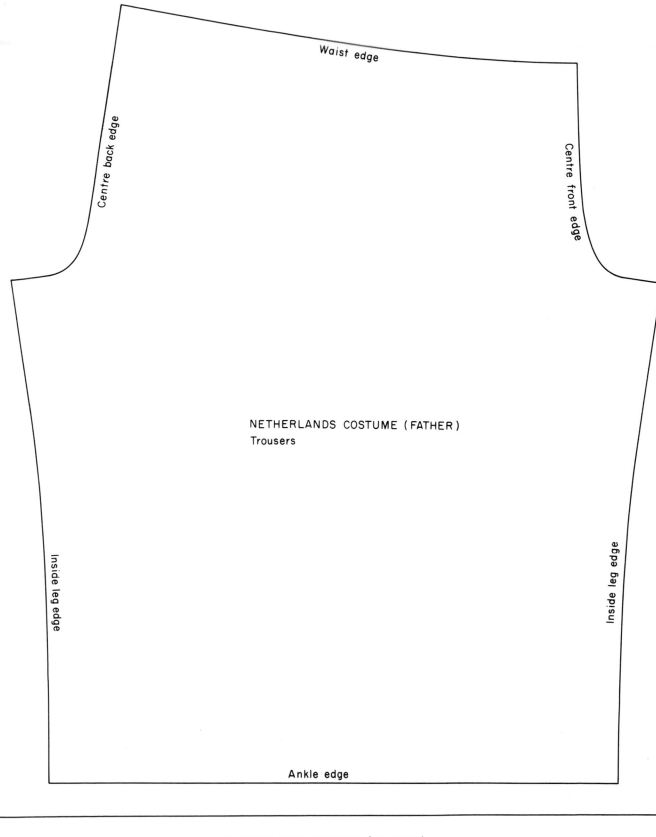

Waist edge

Centre back edge

Centre front edge

NETHERLANDS COSTUME (FATHER)
Trousers

Inside leg edge

Inside leg edge

Ankle edge

NETHERLANDS COSTUME (FATHER)
Trouser waistband

108

Netherlands child costume
Volendam

The little girl wears a lace cap just like her mother's. The dress is light blue and the apron blue and white striped fabric.

Doll

Make the doll by the same method as for the basic female doll with legs, using the following measurements to make a smaller figure. Use a 6 cm (2¼ in.) quarter circle for the body cone and a 5 cm by 10 cm (2 in. by 4 in.) strip of card for each leg. Roll the leg strips up around a knitting needle to make them thinner, noting that the 10 cm (4 in.) measurement is the length of the leg. Shape the ankle slightly as for the adult dolls. Make the head slightly smaller and make it round rather than oval in shape. Mark on the eyes half way down the face and if the face is to be needle-modelled, make only a tiny nose and indent the eyes slightly. Stick a little hair to the forehead.

For each arm fold one pipe cleaner in half and if needle-modelled hands are to be made, omit the extra pipe cleaner for the thumb. Push the ends of one folded pipe cleaner through the card cone and lap it over the other pipe cleaner about 1 cm (⅜ in.). Twist the lapped pipe cleaners together then adjust to make the arms even lengths. Pad out the arms and hands then use the child's arm pattern to make the arm covering in the same way as for the adult dolls. Needle-model the fingers if desired, then take an extra stitch around the hand to make the thumb. Tie a thread around each wrist.

Socks

Make these as given for the mother using the child's sock pattern.

Clogs

Make as for the mother's to the actual sizes shown in diagram 60.

Dress

Use light blue fabric. Cut out the bodice placing the edge of the pattern indicated to a fold in the fabric. Cut the bodice open at the centre front. Turn in and stick the sleeve edges to neaten then join the underarm and side edges. Put the bodice on the doll and overlap and stick the front edges.

For the skirt cut a 9 cm by 30 cm (3½ in. by 12 in.) strip of fabric. Stitch a small tuck in the fabric about 3 cm (1¼ in.) away from one long edge, then sew

a strip of very narrow black braid to the tuck. Turn in the long edge nearest to the tuck and stick to neaten for the hem. Join the short edges of the skirt then run a gathering thread round the remaining raw edge. Put the skirt on the doll, pull up the gathers round the waist and fasten off.

Apron

Use blue and white striped fabric having the stripes running in the direction shown in the illustration. Cut out the apron top placing the edge indicated on the pattern to a fold in the fabric. Cut the apron top open at the centre back. Turn in these centre back edges and stick to neaten, then turn in and stick the side edges. Put the apron top on the doll and stick the waist edges in place at the front and back.

For the apron skirt, cut a 7 cm by 12 cm (2¾ in. by 4¾ in.) strip of fabric. Turn in and stick all the edges except for one 12 cm (4¾ in.) edge. Gather this edge to fit the front waist of the doll then stick it in place lapping it slightly over the raw edge of the apron top.

For the waistband cut a 2 cm (¾ in.) wide strip of fabric long enough to go around the doll's waist. Turn in and stick the long edges to neaten then glue the band round the doll's waist lapping and sticking the short edges at the centre back.

Scarf

For this use a 12 cm (4¾ in.) length of narrow multi-coloured braid or a similar strip of fabric. Fray out the ends to make a fringe then tie the scarf round the doll's neck as illustrated, to cover the raw edges of the neck of the dress and apron.

Lace cap

Using the pattern make the lace cap in exactly the same way as given for the mother's.

The wooden doll

Use a wooden bead 1 cm (⅜ in.) in diameter for the doll's head. Into the bead stick a 3 cm (1¼ in.) length of pipe cleaner. Wrap a little stuffing round this then draw on the face and glue on a little hair as shown in the illustration. Cut a small square of fabric for a shawl and fray out the edges. Fold corner to corner and wrap the shawl around the doll, sticking the folds in place.

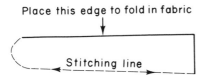

Place this edge to fold in fabric

Stitching line

NETHERLANDS COSTUME (CHILD)
Child's arm pattern

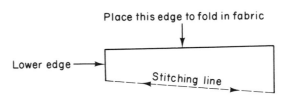

Place this edge to fold in fabric

Lower edge →

Stitching line

NETHERLANDS COSTUME (CHILD)
Child's sock pattern

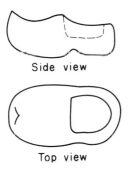

Side view

Top view

Diagram 60
Child's clog, actual size

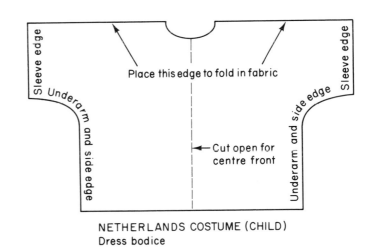

Sleeve edge

Underarm and side edge

Place this edge to fold in fabric

Cut open for centre front

Underarm and side edge

Sleeve edge

NETHERLANDS COSTUME (CHILD)
Dress bodice

Place this edge to fold in fabric

Side edge

Side edge

Cut open for centre back

Waist edge

NETHERLANDS COSTUME (CHILD)
Apron top

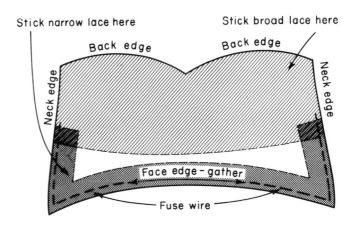

Stick narrow lace here

Stick broad lace here

Back edge

Back edge

Neck edge

Neck edge

Face edge – gather

Fuse wire

NETHERLANDS COSTUME (CHILD)
Lace cap shape

111

Bibliography

Pearl Binder, *The Pearlies*, Jupiter Books (London) Ltd

Angela Bradshaw, *World Costumes*, Adam & Charles Black

Costume Accessories Series, Vols 1–8, B T Batsford Ltd

Georgine de Courtais, *Women's Headdress and Hairstyles in England*, B T Batsford Ltd

Elizabeth Ewing, *History of Twentieth Century Fashion*, B T Batsford Ltd

Lilla M Fox, *Folk Costumes of Southern Europe*, Chatto & Windus

Lilla M Fox, *Folk Costumes of Western Europe*, Chatto & Windus

Lilla M Fox, *Costumes and Customs of the British Isles*, Chatto & Windus

Lepage-Medvey, *National Costumes*, The Hyperion Press

Kathleen Mann, *Peasant Costumes in Europe*, Vols 1 and 2, A & C Black

Anna-Maja Nylen, *Swedish Peasant Costume*, Nordiska Museet

Alma Oakes and Margot Hamilton Hill, *Rural Costume: Its Origin and Development in Western Europe and the British Isles*, B T Batsford Ltd

Kathleen Primmer, *Scandinavian Peasant Costume*, A & C Black

Mary Pringle, *Modern Eskimos*, Franklin Watts

Marion Sichel, *Costume Reference Series*, Vols 1–10, *Roman Britain to the Present Day*, B T Batsford Ltd

R Turner Wilcox, *Dictionary of Costume*, B T Batsford Ltd

R Turner Wilcox, *Five Centuries of American Costume*, Charles Scribner's Sons, New York

R Turner Wilcox, *Folk and Festival Costume of the World*, B T Batsford Ltd

Doreen Yarwood, *Encyclopaedia of World Costume*, B T Batsford Ltd

Doreen Yarwood, *English Costume from the Second Century BC to the Present Day*, B T Batsford Ltd

Doreen Yarwood, *European Costume*, B T Batsford Ltd

Doreen Yarwood, *Outline of English Costume*, B T Batsford Ltd

Some of the books listed above are now out of print but public libraries may have copies or be able to obtain them.

Photographs of national and folk costume can also be found in travel brochures, and magazines such as the *National Geographic*. Central lending libraries may keep back numbers of the *National Geographic* together with indexes covering several years' copies, and these give details of any photographs of costume. Geography books written for children are also usually well illustrated and contain costume photographs.